Conclusion

Furthermore, the information that can be found within the pages described forthwith shall be considered both accurate and truthful when it comes to the recounting of facts. As such, any use, correct or incorrect, of the provided information will render the Publisher free of responsibility as to the actions taken outside of their direct purview. Regardless, there are zero scenarios where the original author or the Publisher can be deemed liable in any fashion for any damages or hardships that may result from any of the information discussed herein.

Additionally, the information in the following pages is intended only for informational purposes and should thus be thought of as universal. As befitting its nature, it is presented without assurance regarding its prolonged validity or interim quality. Trademarks that are mentioned are done without written consent and can in no way be considered an endorsement from the trademark holder.

Introduction

Congratulations on purchasing *Social Media Marketing for Beginners* and thank you for doing so.

The following chapters will discuss several topics related to getting started on the world's hottest social media platforms. For many people, the idea of growing an account from scratch can seem daunting. This is even worse when you are surrounded by larger accounts and it feels impossible to reach their status.

However, I am here to fill you in on all the secrets you need to know regarding social media. This is not a field you need a college degree in. In fact, that is the last place I would recommend you go to. Textbooks are outdated, and most professors are too old to have much experience in social media. The best way to get started is to jump right into it and begin doing your research.

You are, of course, taking a step in that direction by giving this specific book a read.

Social media does not have to be scary. I am going to go over multiple different channels so that you have a full range of knowledge and understand the process for each. The best practices available are right here in this book! I will cover all of the major social media platforms:

- *Instagram*
- *Snapchat*
- *Twitter*
- *YouTube*
- *Facebook*
- *LinkedIn*

It is not just businesses or professionals who are using social media to market, however. These days, anybody can bring in passive revenue, and other great perks, just by cultivating a following on Instagram. This is done through a variety of different marketing practices, all of which are contained in the coming   chapters.

I want to get right into the subject matter, however, so let us hop right to it.

There are plenty of books on this subject on the market, thanks again for choosing this one! Every effort was made to ensure it is full of as much useful information as possible, please enjoy it!

Chapter 1: What s Social Media?

Your Full Explanation on the Details Behind Social Media on the Whole

Exploring the World of Social Networking Platforms

First off, I should probably explain to you what social media platforms are. I know a lot of you are confused as to what these apps and websites are even meant to do. There is a lot of buzz surrounding all of these big names, especially in the younger generation. Because of the quick development of technology, access to social media and the internet has skyrocketed. Almost everybody now has a smartphone ready to go at a moment's notice.

It is because of this that social media influencing was born, and why companies became so fixated on cultivating a presence on these platforms. The widespread usage of social media means getting unlimited access to who you are trying to market to. It also means being able to target the exact demographic you want using crucial analytics.

So, what are these big names? Below, I am going to explain each of these platforms and what they do. I think a good start is to make sure you understand each of them individually, on a superficial level, at least. I will go in-depth on each one through the coming chapters. For now, here is what you need to know:

- **Instagram:** This was originally intended to be a photography app. The creator made it because he wanted a place to share his vintage, Polaroid photography on a massive scale. Needless to say, he never expected it to take off in this way.

  Instagram is easily the hottest platform right now for marketing. Whether you are looking to expand your business or build a following for sponsorships, Instagram is perfect for the job. It allows you to share interactive stories with each other, build a beautiful aesthetic, and get direct feedback from customers.

  Their analytics suite is no joke, either. All around, Instagram is a win for consumers, content creators, and business owners alike!

- **Snapchat:** While not quite as hot as it used to be, Snapchat is making a comeback. Many creators will use it as a way to connect on a more personal level with their followers. There are also news outlets featured, among other things. Snapchat has recently put in games, too, that you can play with a group of people.

This app allows you to share snippets of your life quickly with friends, family, and fans. It is a great way to show them quick clips of your daily life or to share thoughts on the go.

- **Twitter:** This, just like Instagram, is a huge industry leader currently. Twitter forces you to put out short, informational tidbits rather than allowing you to share large statuses. This makes getting information out a lot simpler and much more efficient. It is great for sending out random bits about your day or to interact directly with people.

For whatever reason, Twitter has become one of the apps of choice for the younger generations. They just cannot get enough and neither can businesses and influencers!

- **YouTube:** One of the oldest platforms, alongside Facebook, YouTube is a content powerhouse. You can upload videos of yourself talking to your audience directly. This is known as "vlogging." Vlogging is one of the best ways to really connect with your fans and attract a following. There are quite a few pieces that go into it, but I will go over that in the chapter dedicated to YouTube!

- **Facebook:** This is arguably the platform that started it all. Facebook is now facing government penalties for the outright monopoly it has grown in the digital hemisphere. Facebook has become an absolutely crucial part of even everyday experiences online. There are many websites that allow you to log in using your Facebook account, which speeds up a lot of processes. This means that instead of making an account, you can simply log-in using Facebook at the click of a button.

  Facebook also holds incredible amounts of data on consumer behavior as personal data. What the future holds for Facebook legally is uncertain. However, what we know right now is that you need Facebook to get anywhere. There are a lot of things to know, so stay tuned for the chapter on Facebook.

- **LinkedIn:** You have either heard of LinkedIn, or you have not. It is very well known and popular in the professional sphere. In fact, it is considered the "Facebook" or professional networking. Many jobs allow you to apply straight from LinkedIn using an easy application button. This is a website that has absolutely dominated the way businesses interact with other businesses, as well as how professionals connect directly with each other.

LinkedIn is crucial for everybody to have if they want to have any sort of professional presence on any of the social media platforms. It allows you to build a network, have skills verified, and prove to the professional world that you are worth hiring or working with.

Now that you have a better understanding of these platforms, I think we should talk a little bit more about the business aspects I mentioned prior. There are countless reasons why most companies have switched focus entirely to social media. In fact, there are countless companies that have started because of social media! It has never before been easier to sell to your customers and to understand the population that buys your products.

First of all, you have an immediate connection to all of your customers, or nearly all of them, right at your fingertips. People check social media constantly, so the chance of them seeing live updates from you is pretty high. This is especially true for platforms like Snapchat and Instagram, where you can easily share an update on the go and have your followers receive it almost instantly. Of course, that requires them to turn on notifications for your account... more on that later!

Here are the biggest reasons you should be using social media to its full extent:

- **You have instant access to your customers.** There is nothing better than knowing that you are going to be able to get into contact with customers at a moment's notice. We have seen a huge surge in the quality of customer care and quality assurance. Negative comments are not just negative anymore; with social media, you have the ability to quickly and openly fix your mistakes and apologize.

  This goes a long way in letting your customers know that you are not only a great company - you are trustworthy, and you will own up to your mistakes. Social media can be a public relations nightmare, however, just as quickly as it can bring fame. Be mindful of what you post and who is in charge of your social media programs.

- **Constant engagement with your brand is a possibility.** The goal is always to get people interacting with you. You want there to be a large community associated with your brand or products. This sense of community develops a strong following of loyal consumers who hang on your every word. Engagement can be drive in several ways with social media. Of course, I will go in-depth on this topic with each of the following chapters.

For now, just know that you can encourage engagement with all of these platforms. LinkedIn is a bit of an exception, but it is an out layer in the way that it has a very specific, niche market. Keep reading for the chapter on this more puzzling piece of social media set-ups!

- **Expanding your reach has never been cheaper.** If you do things correctly, making sure your social media takes off can be cheap or free. Any small amount of overhead that you incur before you bring in revenue is inconsequential, as well. This is because of all of the tools social media provides to reach out to people. No matter who you are, you can build a following and launch merch or products because of it.

Many businesses have been started simply as a result of social media. You do not need to begin as an expert in order to succeed in this field. You just need to do some solid research - like reading this book!

- **Social media use is taking the world by storm.** There are millions and millions of people keeping touch across multiple different platforms. Part of the reason that it is so important to cultivate a following on all of them is that you are able to reach more audiences. There are distinct crowds who tend to hang around each of the platforms. Of course, many will use multiple apps or websites, but most have that specific one that they prefer.

  It is because of this that you need to jump on this hot marketing tool. The access directly to people has never been more achievable. This makes marketing a snap if you know how to do it! Of course, you will be an expert by the concluding chapter, so get ready for your imminent success.

- **Keeping tabs on what is hot and on-trend has never been easier.** Even if you are part of an older generation, which is likely the case, you can easily keep track of what is happening in the world. I recommend keeping up with YouTube, especially since this is a great news source in many ways. There are multiple channels that go over local, world, and entertainment news in a much more candid and honest way.

  On top of this, you have great access to videos, posts, and

more on any social media platform. Finding members of your target audience who are already influencers is a power that you need to put into play. This is crucial market research which will give you the power to more accurately appeal to these target audiences.

- **Analytics allow for an incredible look into buying habits, and more.** I know I have talked up the suite of analytics that will be available to you. However, even if you are not a marketing professional currently, I think you can understand the importance of them. Analytics is the best tool you have for absolutely every single part of your marketing plan. These numbers and pieces of data will not only impact your social media plans and schedule, but it will also help you in every avenue of your business   plan.

Any time you can get raw data on your target markets and audience, you need to take complete advantage. This will help you begin to cater to your brand's voice and style to these people so that you can better appeal to them.

It is not just about keeping tabs on your potential clients and leads. It is about reaching out and making sure that you are using the best marketing practices in order to keep them coming back. There is nothing better for doing this than a traditional marketing funnel.

Marketing funnels can also be called sales funnels. However, to keep things consistent, I will only be using the term marketing funnel.

There are several different types of the marketing funnel. Most businesses and brands will actually tweak it to create their own based on their needs. Social media funnels are a little bit different, as well, on top of this general need for tweaking. This presents new problems, but it also presents a lot of great solutions. Making sure your marketing funnel is up to par is not too hard. Below, I am going to go over two different types of the funnel: one catered to business on the whole, as well as one I suggest using for social media.

First, let me explain a couple of pieces of terminologies, so you do not get confused with all the lingo:

- **Converted/Conversion:** This is the act of getting somebody to complete some portion of your marketing funnel. However, it can be used in a few ways. For now, we are just using it to mean moving somebody from one part of your plan to the next. This can be going to your website, visiting your page, etc.

- **Cold Lead:** This is a potential client or customer. When you run an advertisement, these are the people who have not yet heard of you. You are trying to convert them.

- **Warm Lead:** A warm lead is somebody who has been converted in some way. They are not yet "closed" on, but they are at least aware of you. They may be following you or a frequenter of your page.

- **Closed:** This is the act of making the final sale or completing the final phase of your marketing funnel. Social media is not just about selling a product. This is the end goal of your business, perhaps, but not for specific marketing related to social media. You could just be getting people to follow you, for example.

- **Call To Action:** Whenever you ask for a lead to do something, it is a call to action. This can be as simple as posting a poll to your story or asking them to visit your website in your bio. The end goal is always to generate engagement through calls to action.

Let me get right down into the info:

General Marketing Funnel Structure

There is a general format when it comes to these funnels. You will learn slightly different ones depending on where you go for the information. Below, I am going to list out the steps in the one that I generally follow as my starting point. Once you are comfortable with the terminology and understand the general process, which should not take long, you can move forward with switching things around until it fits.

1. **Untouched:** This is your pool of candidates for your marketing techniques. You can call them "cold leads."

2. **Contact Made:** Once you have reached out and made your cold leads aware of you, you have moved into the phase where contact has been made. It is now up to you to make them want to continue that contact.

3. **Lead Landed:** Now that they have moved on to the next part, you have landed your lead. It is from here that you want to begin presenting your end goal to the potential client or consumer. Or, at this point, your warm lead.

4. **Proposal Presented:** Beginning to present your proposal will snowball into serious calls to action.

5. **Negotiation:** This really only happens with those who are negotiating prices with potential customers or clients. This is the stage in a car sale, for example, where prices are haggled.

6. **Closing:** You have finally gotten to the final stage. This is the best part where you get to close the sale! It is time to celebrate.

Now that you understand this general set up, I am going to go ahead and make sure that you have a great starting point for your social media business or brand.

Social Media Marketing Funnel Structure

I want you to understand the first model in order to better tackle other aspects of your business. However, because of the topic of this book, it is probably expedient to give you one more suited to social media on the whole. I think you will find that this well-established technique will clear up any problems you have. It clearly explains every step and keeps you on task for what comes next.

Here is the set-up I suggest, alongside an explanation of it:

1. **Strategize:** You first need to come up with your strategy and what you are looking to do. This will be when you decide to run an advertisement, start a sale promotion, host a contest; whatever you can dream up!

2. **Customize:** Once you have decided which path you are going to head down, you need to begin customizing it. This is where you will decide who the target market is and what designs you need for the campaign at hand.

3. **Analyze:** Understanding your analytics and putting them into play is a huge part of this funnel. This step will take the longest as you go through and start to understand what your analytics are saying.

4. **Land Leads:** Once you have made them aware of you, you have made contact. They are not yet following you or purchasing from your sales page, generally speaking. But you have at least made contact with them even in the most basic way. This is when you will begin attempting to land that lead. This is the most tricky part of it!

5. **Engage:** From here, you will move into the phase where you are proposing something to them. This is where your calls to action come into play. You are presenting to them a proposal of engagement and trying to get them to answer positively to it.

6. **Convert:** Once you get the person to follow you, or even click over and like your photos, you have landed them as a potential lead. This is why you need to make sure you are following people who interact with you early on and answer them. Making sure you are staying on top of following up with comments, DMs, etc. is key in landing a lead.

7. **Retarget:** I will go over this in-depth later. For this reason, I will not really touch on it here. For now, just know that this is the act of targeting ads to people who have already answered a call to action.

8. **Finalize:** This is the stage in which a person will finalize the sale, or subscribe to your newsletter, or whatever else you are trying to make happen.

The main reason this looks so different is because of the vastly different aspects related to social media. This is an entirely different market that people are still getting used to. We are still paving out the road to understanding how best to market for social media. Of course, some of us are a little ahead of the curve than others. After reading this, you will be one of those lucky few!

This all relies on having a strong marketing plan for your content, however. Content marketing is a type of marketing all on its own. This is for good reason! It has become the number one way in order to get things done on social media and the internet as a whole. Your "content" refers to anything that you produce. This refers to the following:

- *Posts*

- *Videos*

- *Blogs*

- *Memes*

- *Ads*

- *... and more!*

I want to go over the concepts behind content marketing so you can begin to understand the ins and outs of content creation. This will really give you a solid baseline for the rest of the book. I want you to know what I am referring to and have a solid understanding of the terminology at play.

After all, you do not want to be the only one in the room who does not know what the other professionals are talking about!

The end result of this is always to cultivate a professional presence through which to gain more passive revenue.

First of all, there is a difference between content "creation" and content "curation." These are both valid parts of content marketing. However, if you really want to gain traction, you need to focus on content creation. Let me go over what they are, exactly, so you have a better understanding:

- **Content Creation:** This is the act of creating your own content. You probably understand that, however, from the name. Any time you write your own posts, create your own memes, or upload original content of any type, you are engaging in content creation.

- **Content Curation:** On the flip side, you can also use the content presented by others. I will explain the etiquette behind doing so on each of the platforms. Make sure that you are not violating any copyrights or plagiarizing others - that is not the goal of content curation!

But which one is best? And how do you even decide where to use them? Both are valid questions you most likely have at this point. Let me go over the pros and cons of both systems. That should allow you to have an easier time deciding which route to go down.

Pros of Content Creation

- **It is original to you.** You can be sure that there is no other account presenting this information in the same way.

- **You can entirely customize it.** Whatever you can think up can be created! You can also add your logo and add any effects you would like.

- **This is a better way to build your brand.** By creating content, you are letting your brand's voice be known to potential leads. It will give you a much stronger brand voice.

- **Generating a following requires great content.** First and foremost, you need to make sure you pack your accounts full of fantastic original content. There are many accounts that only repost, but these are not accounts that generate revenue. Original content is the best way to get that following growing.

Cons of Content Creation

- **It takes a lot of time.** Unfortunately, there is no way around it. If you are looking to create great, compelling content, it is going to take you some time.

- **You may not have the skills to do it.** This is part of the reason why most companies are now employing social media marketing consultants. Larger companies generally have an entire suite of professionals in the social media arena.

These creative teams are indispensable for their knowledge in different areas of content creation. You will need to build your skillset in many ways in order to create your content.

Pros of Content Curation

- **Curation allows for more engagement.** Because you are reposting somebody else's content, you can easily tag them in it. They will most likely repay this by reposting it and saying thank-you or engaging with your content more. It allows for easier reach to more accounts in a more personal manner.

- **Viral marketing usually starts with curating great, unknown content.** If you are especially talented at talent scouting, you can find content that is unknown. There are a lot of things out there that could easily go viral. Once you have amassed a following, it is easier to do this. Plus, when that account blows up, they will remember you!

- **This can help you build connections on the network.** When you are reposting things, make sure you also repost from large accounts. This will give you a starting point to begin cultivating a relationship. That is the first step in finding sponsors or influencers to work with!

Cons of Content Curation

- **It can backfire sometimes.** If you do not do it properly, it may be seen as "stealing." This is a huge problem. You also may find that some accounts do not appreciate their content being re-used. Just make sure you use common sense and respect people's boundaries regarding their content.

- **It makes you look less original.** As mentioned, having a grid of purely reposted content is going to do little for you. You want to be original and make sure you are offering something nobody else is. Stick to sharing relevant curated content. Just because it is funny or interesting does not mean that it belongs to your account or relates to your brand.

Hopefully, you now have a better handle on the differences between the two. I am hoping that you will have an easier time understanding which method will be right for which situation.

It is time to move on to my final thoughts on this topic before we move into more on creating content!

I would now like to touch on the general etiquette of content curation. I think that it is only fair for me to set you up for success in this endeavor. After all, you do not want to fall into the trap of social media anger by ripping off other creators. That is a great way to get the majority of the platform to turn on you pretty quickly!

Original content is, by far, what you should be relying on the most. For different platforms, the level of necessity will change, but overall, it is fairly consistent. You want to use this as much as possible in order to gain your following. Creating original content does not have to be as hard as it seems. There are a number of apps and other programs I will go over shortly to help you do just that.

First, you want to begin to cultivate your aesthetic. This simply means the overarching theme of your account and what all of the imagery looks like. You will need to also cultivate a voice, which will relate to the copy that you write. Doing so requires a lot of thought and time. You do not want to jump right into sharing your stuff or getting your account off of the ground. Instead, focus on getting your aesthetic together, so it is consistent from the very beginning.

Figuring out your branded image is not a simple task. It may be easier if you already have an established business or a solid business plan or vision. However, starting from scratch means that you need to build it from the ground up. Try and brainstorm what your brand is going to stand for. I recommend getting out a good, old pen and pad of paper. Write down words that encompass your brand and what you are all about. Begin to think about colors you like, logos, and all of that good stuff.

You will figure it out given a little time!

There are a few apps that can help you begin to bring this voice and brand to life. I really want to make sure that you are aware of the tools at your disposal. These tools will carry you through all of your interactions on the different social media platforms. You will find that having a few apps on your phone can open up far different avenues and help you get to the point where you are creating stunning content.

Below, I will go over each of the apps I suggest you download. I will give you the cost of their premium versions, as well, and whether or not I think it is worth investing.

Here we go!

- **Unfold:** If you want to create gorgeous stories easily, Unfold is the go-to for many brands. It gives you some great templates for story posts and allows you to fully customize them. This is one of the best apps out there to make sure your story is on point every time.

  Premium Price: $15/yr

  Is It Worth It: In my experience, the Unfold premium just is not worth it. Sure, there are some cool templates, but you will do just fine using the ones provided on the free version. You will, of course, have to weigh your options and figure out what is right for you. This is just my opinion!

- **VSCO:** Editing photos can be a pain, especially when it comes to doing it on your computer. Luckily, you do not have to. VSCO allows for making gorgeous edits to coloring, as well as a slew of other features. This powerful tool has become highly popular, and for good reason.

Premium   **Price:** $20/yr

Is It Worth It: Absolutely. VSCO is the best editing app on the market currently. Their pro features are incredible and they even let you add those filters to videos! You should definitely be prioritizing VSCO's premium subscription over others. This is especially true if you will be doing video content.

- **Mojo:** This is another app that is fantastic for story creation. It should be used in conjunction with Unfold. It offers amazing animation and effects. However, it does not offer regular text, so Unfold should be used more heavily.

Premium   **Price:** $40/yr

Is It Worth It: This depends on where you are with your business. If you are really moving towards posting engaging content constantly and are bringing in revenue, you should definitely invest. Mojo is a great app, but you do not need to use it all the time at first.

- **Pexels:** Royalty-free stock photos are a pain to find. Pexels offers a fantastic selection of different photos you are free and clear to use, even commercially!

  There is no premium version of Pexels. Adobe Stock is a great resource if you want access to more specific photos and a lot more variety of it.

You will find multiple different apps that help you on your journey. These are just a handful to get you on your feet. Countless programs exist on the app front, but there are great websites, as well as programs for your computer. It is all about making sure you are using all of the resources at your disposal.

So, what are the best programs to be using? I am going to list three, which have become industry standards. You will want to make sure you are using at least a couple in order to fully take advantage of social media. Posting daily and interacting can suck up a lot of your time.

But, hey, more on solving that below:

- **HootSuite:** This is the industry standard for organizing, scheduling, and sharing content. It also allows you to easily curate topics and articles which are customized for you specifically. The analytics suite is also powerful and offers a lot in the way of understanding your audience. HootSuite is a great resource for anybody looking to up their social media game.

  Premium Price: $45/mth

  Is It Worth It: Once you understand analytics and you are really pushing forward on the social media front, it is a great idea to invest in HootSuite. However, you do not want to pay this huge price until you are bringing in the amount of money to justify it.

- **Buffer:** Another method of scheduling social media posts, Buffer is another industry-standard program. It has a different format than HootSuite, and it does not offer quite as much. However, it is much more beginner-friendly and a great starting point. It also offers some great analytics and other features.

Premium   **Price:** $15/mth

- **Is It Worth It:** This is a lot more affordable than HootSuite. Honestly, I recommend investing in Buffer right off of the bat. The ability to schedule your posts and keep your media constantly updated is invaluable. The free versions limit your ability to schedule content, which puts a huge hamper on your ability to be consistent and constant on the platform.

- **MailChimp:** If you are looking to release a newsletter, you need a program to do it with. They are easy to put together if you understand what you are doing. This is not a book on MailChimp, however, or newsletters. For that reason, I will not get too much into it! Just know that this is your starting point for launching anything e-mail related.

Premium   **Price:** $10/mth

- **Is It Worth It:** Without a doubt! MailChimp is the best way to send out e-mails and make sure you are hitting your target market. E-mail campaigns are more and more important as people become more closely tied to their phones. Social media provides a fantastic way to request people's e-mails to your campaigns.

Now that I have covered the very basics behind this marketing, I think it is high time to get into the meat of the matter. I am going to focus on different social media platforms in each of the following chapters. Feel free to skip around in order to get the information on the platform you are currently setting up!

The first platform we are going to explore is the contender for a top place among all social media apps. Yes, this includes Facebook! Speaking of which, this company is actually owned by Facebook. Many people do not know that. Keep reading to find out what else you do not know about Instagram, the first platform I am going to reach you about.

Chapter 2: Instagram

Everything You Need to Know About How to Master Instagram

There are several reasons you want to use Instagram. In fact, I would argue there are none at all against the idea. Instagram is one of the best apps to have and one which is in use by a majority of the world. It is the favored platform for younger generations, as well, and has birthed the entire idea of hiring Influencers as your marketing specialists on these platforms.

The way TV advertising is quickly declining. People are choosing more and more to put their money into different avenues in order to increase revenue and find new leads. The rate at which other types of advertising is declining is astonishing. Social media has paved the way to freedom from the big screen, and most people are going towards streaming services. YouTube actually offers an alternative to TV, but I will get into that in a later chapter.

For now, I want to talk about the reasons that Instagram is taking the world by storm. More specifically, I would like to go over the reasons why you cannot keep from getting involved with this platform.

Let me go over the biggest reasons below:

- **It is the go-to choice for the younger generation.** There is no bigger platform, besides, perhaps, Twitter, which calls to the younger generation. This is the group of people with the most purchasing power, generally speaking. Teenagers and young adults are always on the look for the next big thing and are the people who sway all   trends.

  Making sure you can reach the younger generation is incredibly important. To stay relevant, you need to know what is going on. Instagram allows you to do this incredibly easy.

- **They have the easiest calls to action that get results.** Want to post a poll? Do it in a snap with Instagram. You can do quizzes, ask questions, and more. If there is a piece of information you want to share or engagement you want to be raised, then Instagram will help   you   do   it.

  On top of this, most of their calls to action come with an analytics suite that gives you more information than you could ever need on that specific call to action. They offer analytics on each and every one of your posts, as well as on your story. This is complemented by the overall view of the analytics they provide in their specific analytics section.

Can I say analytics more? Actually, I can, because that is the next reason!

- **Their analytic suite is no joke.** As mentioned above, they have an incredible analytics suite which has a host of information you need. Instagram gives you easy access to the stats on all of your posts, as well as a solid view of the numbers associated with your story.

Out of all of the platforms, Instagram absolutely has the most powerful analytics suite. This is part of the reason that it is the best one to start off on. Everything is easy to understand. It can be a great way to learn about analytics and what they can do for you.

- **It is connected with Facebook.** This has some serious perks! However, there are a few downfalls to it. Unfortunately, you cannot run ads on Instagram unless you are connected to Facebook. For most, this is not a problem; however, some people stay off of Facebook on purpose.

If you are looking to be an influencer, you need to bite the bullet and stay on Facebook. You really cannot escape this marketing giant, even as you try to escape to a different platform!

- **Branding yourself is incredibly easy.** The fact that you can design your grid however you would like is hugely beneficial to showing off the specific style of your brand. You want to make sure that voice rings clear and true through all of your social media. Instagram allows you to very clearly define yourself so that you have an easier time moving over to other places.

On other platforms, it can be difficult to see the "whole picture," so to speak. What I mean by this is seeing all of the imagery and how it correlates. On Instagram, it is all right there in front of you. You can see all of the images clearly, side by side, and that allows you to more easily stay consistent in your designs and imaging.

- **You can provide links and great info...** all at the tap of a finger. The highlights icons are fantastic for making sure that all of the important info is available. This is an ingenious move on Instagram's part and is now a huge selling point for salespeople. Highlights icons can be used for so many different things, all of which I'll go over later!

These are just a few reasons, there are many more! I will begin to get more into them as we delve into Instagram and how, exactly, to get started on it.

So, how do you start setting up your content? The first thing I would suggest is to do some market research. You want to look into your own niche and see who is doing what. First, create your account. Use your brand's username. If you have to deviate because the name is taken, try adding an underscore or a period in it.

Now that you are on the platform, start poking around. Do not be scared to leave your profile blank for a while as you cultivate the information you need. Follow people who seem to have the same ideas and whose content you like. These will be people you will want to build relationships with once you are up and running. You are basically setting up the skeleton for the rest of your interactions on Instagram.

One of the most important things to do while doing this is to make sure you are taking a good, long look at what hashtags are being used. You want to use somewhere between 10-15 hashtags for Instagram. Use a mix of high-volume ones (those with 1mill+ posts), and low-volume ones (those with less than 1mill posts). This allows you to access the large tags but not be swallowed up by them. The smaller ones will help your posts be seen, but the big ones obviously have a lot of draws, too.

Try and seek out which hashtags are being used the most in that specific community. You can do this by noting the recurring ones you are seeing on all of your favorite accounts. You will want to cultivate three different groups of hashtags. You will cycle through each of these in order to expand your reach. All three groups should have entirely different hashtags in them for this purpose.

Now, you need to start thinking about your actual grid. Cultivating a fantastic grid does not have to be a huge pain. You can easily use any of the programs or websites I mentioned earlier in order to do this. If you are a business owner, you may want to hire some specialists in the field. Freelance designers are easy to find. Even if you are not a business and you are just trying to create passive revenue, you still may want to look into this.

Believe it or not, paying artists for designs is actually not going to break the bank. Some of them will do your icons for as little as

$20. This is a pretty great price for something entirely unique to you and customized to your tastes.

Follow these steps when thinking about your grid:

- **Are you going to schedule these posts?** You have two options. You can either post all of them yourself, or you can load them into one of the systems I recommended. Buffer and HootSuite are powerful tools for this, but there are some things you need to consider first, like the entry below this!

- **Do you want to do large, multi-post grids?** One of the biggest trends right now is taking a large image and splitting it up, so that instead of each square is its own image, the entire image takes up six squares. This is a great tactic for doing a "bold," "in your face" campaign. I normally do not trust systems with these larger grids. I want to be there for the live upload so that if anything goes wrong, it can be fixed immediately.

  The issue with this style of the grid is simply that there are many ways to go wrong. If you upload even one photo out of order, you may have to delete four to fix it.

- **How often do you plan on posting?** There are different posting schedules suggested for different niches. You need to figure out what your target audience wants and expects. Generally, daily posts are recommended at the very least. You do not want people to lose track of you or to forget about you because you are not popping up in their feed.

- **What color scheme are you going to use?** There are a ton of different programs I suggested which can help you edit your photos. You need to figure out which filter you are using, and which presets, and stick to them. Part of making sure your brand and grid are cohesive is sticking to the same theme the whole way down.

Once you have answered these questions, get right down into creating your content. I recommend posting three times a day using your analytics to determine when. You can do this by viewing the "Audience" section in your analytics suite and scrolling all the way down.

Now that your grid is sorted out and you have an idea of the content you are posting, move on to your icon and highlight icons. There are a ton of different things you can use for your highlights. Here are some ideas:

- An "About You" section
- A section for your sponsors
- Vacation or travel
- Contests
- ... and more!

Basically, anything interesting that you want people to be able to access at a glance should go here. Your highlights will only consist of story posts, however, since technically, they are "story highlights." Just keep that in mind!

Finally, after you have your account set up and loaded with a little content, you want to begin interacting with others. This is the main goal of social media. You need to begin to explore the other accounts in your niche to alert them to your presence. Share other people's posts to your story, comment, like... do all of those great things social media allow us to do!

Once you are up and running, you need to begin thinking about ads. There is a huge debate as to whether or not ads are a good investment, and in a lot of cases, they may not be on Instagram. There are several different factors that can come into play here. You will want to keep a tight handle on your analytics and research a lot into how all of those numbers work before you even think about paying for an ad slot or promotion.

Setting up an Instagram ad campaign is pretty easy. You will actually be doing it through Facebook since that is the company that owns Instagram now. Each post of yours will allow you to "promote" it, which simply means to make an ad for it. You will just tap that and follow the prompts! Part of the reason I love Instagram is that everything is so easy to do, and you really do not need to be an expert to operate it.

There are a few things to keep in mind for Instagram ads. Here are some of the best practices to keep in mind:

- **Use the same terminology.** Do you start every post telling your followers they're "super rad"? Then, make sure you use that phrase in your ad! If you are prone to using certain words or have catchphrases, use it to draw in the audience and to appeal to those who may already be familiar with it. It is all about staying consistent!

- **Be consistent with your voice.** Speaking of being consistent, you want everything to match. Not just with your grid, but for the ad campaign itself. All of the imagery should be fairly consistent and different from the regular grid images. They should match, but should stand out as their own "thing."

- **Use the special features of Instagram.** There are a ton of features, like Boomerang, which allows you to make cool ads. This is even truer when it comes to sharing ads to the story.

- **Check your analytics.** You want to make sure you are posting in the right demographic and setting everything accordingly. Make sure you use your analytics to determine the times the ad should run, which audiences should be targeted, etc. Do not just use your Instagram analytics, however. Take the data from your different platforms if you can!

Speaking of which, let us talk a little about the two different ways you can make an ad.

- **Story:** If you were not aware, Instagram now allows you to run ads in the Story section. This is a great way to get people engaged quickly. It is almost an answer to TV or radio ads that people can choose to skip over. The key is making them so interesting that they do not, in fact, skip over it. That comes down to your designing and marketing, however!

- **Feed:** This is the way you are probably most familiar with. Feed ads will go right into somebody's home feed.

They blend right into the rest of the images, which is a huge advantage. If your content is right on par with what they like, they will most likely click over and check you out.

Those are the two ways to get your ad campaign going in the right direction!

The best way to encourage movement towards gaining passive revenue, or selling products, is by growing slowly and organically. Sure, you can buy followers, but that is not going to help you in the long run. In fact, it could end up hurting you. This is against the ToS (Terms of Service) set by every social media platform. You can get in a lot of hot water, and even have your account terminated.

Also, people are not stupid. They can see your account and know that you bought those followers. This makes you look insincere and even narcissistic. They do not want to follow somebody who just wants to look successful without doing all of the hard work that makes that happen.

Here are the best ways to get that organic, slow growth moving along:

- **Follow Others:** Make sure that you are following proper etiquette. For different platforms, it is different. On Instagram, it is nice to do, but you do not have to follow back. I suggest doing so for the first few hundred followers, however. Remember that you never want to follow and then unfollow a ton of people to increase your following. Again, people are not stupid and they will notice this. It is a great way to make a lot of people angry!

- **Interact in the Community:** You do not want to just follow people. That is awesome, but it will not really start conversations or start conversions. You need to make sure that you are actively commenting on and liking other people's photos. Interact on their stories and make sure they know that you exist.

- **Create Mini Contests:** Popping a mini-contest into your story, or even onto your grid, encourages people to interact with you. Make sure you create low entry requirements and give a shout out to those who join in!

- **Feature Other Accounts:** One of the best ways to bring attention to yourself is by sharing the photos of others. You can do this by putting them on your grid but be careful if you do. Some people do not allow reposting. Just make sure to check their accounts to make sure they are not.

49

Making sure that you are growing properly is not hard. You will find that the more effort you put in right at the very beginning, the better. Eventually, your account will grow to the point where you can start backing off. This is because the followers will start flowing in without you having to do a whole lot. It is at this point that you should move to another platform and begin growing there.

You may want to begin working with Influencers at this point. This will help you expand your reach far more quickly. It can be pricey doing this, however, so keep that in mind. You may be able to sweeten the deal by doing a giveaway and providing all of the products for it. Generally, however, you are still paying somebody upward of $100 in order to work with you. This is a better way to spend your money, however, than on ads. Influencers are, without a doubt, the best way to get yourself out there as quickly as possible.

You will want to make sure that you understand analytics. This goes far deeper than just those that are attached to your account. Phlanx is a great website you can use in order to pull both your analytics, as well as the analytics of others. You will need to do a lot of research into these numbers. There are entire books based on it, and unfortunately, I do not have the time to explain analytics for all the different platforms. Just know that when you continue your education, this is your first priority!

There are many different ways to find influencers. You can use any of the following avenues:

- **Phlanx:** This is a great place to go in order to have analytics pulled for any number of platforms. You want to go here before you decide to work with anybody. They have engagement calculators but keep in mind you can only look up the engagement for three accounts a day if you do not have a subscription.

- **Instagram:** Of course, you could always just browse Instagram! If you did the first steps correctly, you should be following some influencers you like already. Do not aim too high unless you have the budget for it but go for those influencers who have a few thousand followers. It will also open up a relationship with them and if they become super popular, you knew them while they were still small creators! There is power in networking.

Most influencers will offer contact information in their bio. If they do not, reach out to them and see if they want to partner up! Some small influencers will not charge for partnerships for contests or giveaways.

- **HypeAuditor:** The number one place to go for free info is HypeAuditor. This is a place where you can see exactly who-is-who with influencing. It provides free rankings complete with explanations and ways to contact the people you want.

All of them provide a great way to get into contact with those that you would be excited to work with. The best way to go is with the cheapest way that still gives you a lot of info. Luckily, you can pretty easily tell which accounts are successful enough for you to feel comfortable paying them. It also helps if they have already had partnerships and sponsors so that you can see what their experience is.

Now that you have gotten everything together, you can begin to polish it all up. There are always going to be loose ends you want to tie back together. If you own a business, you may look into hiring a specialist to help you. This will become truer as you develop an audience. Eventually, it will become too much work to do all by yourself. Most influencers have an entire team of people that help them handle their messages, upload their content, polish up videos, and more. It is kind of like being a celebrity! After all, influencers are the modern age socialites.

There are some good parts and bad parts of hiring an influencer. Let us go over some of these below.

Pros of Hiring a Specialist

- **They are, well, specialized!** You will probably want to hire somebody who specifically specializes in an area you are bad in. Video editing, for example, is an area most people are weak in. In order to make sure yours are up to par, make sure you are going through an official editor. This goes for just about anything you may be weak on, however, including editing photos and doing basic photography.

- **There is less stress on you.** When you can hand over the reins to somebody else, there is far less stress involved. Unfortunately, becoming successful in social media gets really stressful very quickly. This is because of the influx of comments, messages, and general notifications. When you do not have to have your phone blowing up all of the time, it is a good thing.

- **PR mistakes are less likely to happen.** Most of us are not experts on people. Even when we like to think we are, there are a lot of things which we miss or are lost in translation. This is the reason for huge outbursts from the public when a marketing professional misstep and says something that is dumb. Somebody who is experienced with marketing and PR will understand how to handle situations that arise and know how to prevent them from happening in the first place.

- **Staying organized becomes easier.** Keeping track of your social media calendar can get hectic! This is part of that stress factor. Most people are not great when it comes to staying on top of things. This is part of the reason that so many books about the organization are written and sold. There are even professional organizers out there!

Cons of Hiring a Specialist

- **They can be pretty pricey.** Whenever you are hiring somebody for their expertise, you can bet that they are going to cost a chunk of change. They have knowledge of the industry and experience working in it. You are paying them for this experience and knowledge. However, the benefits are absolutely uncountable!

- **You may not like working with them.** Not the person but working with them in the capacity of creative development. A lot of people have trouble letting go and allowing another person to take hold of where their social media is going. This is especially true when you have built yourself up from the bottom.

Once you have decided whether you want to work with a specialist or not, you can move onwards to the next step. Those who are going to hire specialists will most likely have that specialist do the next steps. However, I want to go over them so that you understand them and for those of you who are going to do it all yourself.

Photography is one of the most important parts. After all, Instagram is at its core a place to share photos and snapshots of your life. The Instagram aesthetic has become widely popularized, but there are quite a few of them. This is why market research is so important. You need to know what other people are doing in the same niche before you decide on what you are going to do. The goal is not to copy others; it is simply ensuring that your brand will be compelling to your target audience.

There are a few best practices for image sizing. I will go over this below for each of the different sizes:

- **Icon:** 180px by 180px

- **Story:** 1080px by 1920px

- **Grid:** 1080px by 1080px

Those are the general guidelines for how large your images should be. Use this as your baseline for creating images. Just make sure that the ratio stays the same if you are going to be working with higher-resolution images.

There are a few photography tips and tricks I want to share with you, as well. Photography can be difficult to get the hang of, but once you start to understand the underlying concepts it will be easier. I suggest doing a lot of research into photography to get started on the right foot, especially with Instagram.

Keep in mind that if you have a nice smartphone, you can do all of this without investing

Photography Tips and Tricks

- **Avoid a shaking camera.** You can buy different pieces of equipment to help with this. I recommend a great tripod that will keep you from getting blurry photos.

- **Avoid using flash.** You can use a paper towel in order to soften flash. This will create blown-out results with poor color quality. Flash should not be used outside at all and should always be softened when used indoors.

- **Invest in some equipment.** Tripods are only one piece of equipment you should look into buying. There are a ton of lenses, even ones you can attach right to your iPhone.

- **Give your photos some depth.** Make sure that you are using props! Make sure that there are other places of focus besides the subject. Instead of photographing yourself in front of the ocean, try to stand beside rocks or get the pier in the photo. Creating depth makes it feel more real to those looking at it.

Photography is not the only part of this, however. We also need to take a good, long, hard look at the current trends and fads happening. As mentioned earlier, large images that span across your grid are currently very popular. These are the trends that you want to keep track of. Some of the biggest trends happening in the market are as follows:

- **Multi-Image Grids:** I have already talked about these quite a bit. This is basically the concept that when you look at a grid, it looks like there is just one large photo.

Many people are using this in interesting ways. Toy with the idea and check out other accounts who are doing it!

- **More Story Posts:** Instagram is absolutely leaning more towards story posts than actually posting to their grid. Of course, you still want to make posts! But keeping your story loaded up and active is becoming way more important.

- **Social Awareness:** Knowing what is going on in the world around us is very much in fashion. People are going towards authenticity rather than trying to look like they are living a perfect life. Mental illness, marginalized populations, and all of the other parts of social justice are becoming more and more something brands are talking about.

- **Long Captions:** No longer are we just putting down something short and simple in captions! It is far more popular now to make sure you are really laying it all out. Make thoughtful posts that are related to the image you are sharing. Put real thought and effort into what you are saying. People are loving long captions these days!

I think this is the best place to leave you with final thoughts! This is the best guide you will ever find on getting started with

Instagram. However, that is only one of the many platforms we are exploring today. The next on the list is the parent company of Instagram. Thumb over to the next chapter so that you can get the skinny on exactly how Facebook works.

Chapter 3: Facebook

What You Need to Do to Grow on Facebook

Is there a person left on earth who has access to the internet but does not have a Facebook account? I honestly do not think there are. While some people have decided to leave the platform over privacy concerns, it still reigns supreme over every other platform out there. However, keep in mind that this is starting to shift. Facebook is the most popular by far because it was started long before any of the others. Instagram was recently introduced in 2018, so it is a baby in comparison. There are many other platforms now and the younger generation is choosing to branch outward as a result.

Facebook still remains the best place to be if you want to get your business going in the right direction and to make sure your ads are hitting target audiences. Their incredible analytics suite allows for absolute control over every single part of where your money is going. There is absolutely no platform out there that has quite the same handle on all of that data. Facebook is a rival even to Google at this point when it comes to data collected on consumers!

As I did before, I am going to start this off with the biggest reasons you should be using Facebook. I will be doing this for every section so you can understand the biggest perks at a glance!

- **Incredible reach to potential customers or clients.** Did you know that there are over 1 billion users on Facebook? That sounds like a crazy number, but it is true. The number of people and the amount of data that Facebook has is unbelievable. I do not think I need to say more about how many people you can reach and how much data you can gather from this platform.

- **Ultimate control over your ads.** Because of the data you have, you can tweak your ads until they are perfect. Facebook also offers a number of different analytics you can adjust during the ad creation process. More on that later in the chapter, however!

- **Low expense in order to get started.** It costs you exactly $0 to get started with your Facebook page. Nothing you do will cost you unless you want to put that money forward. The best part about social media is the low cost of entry. Facebook is no exception.

- **An understanding of your target audience.** Beyond this, again, you know exactly who they are. You even know what they are interested in besides your own products or services. There is no better way to get a handle on who is watching you than keeping track of what is going on with your Facebook analytics.

- **Website traffic will increase exponentially.** Because Facebook is still popularly used on the computer, you can easily get people clicking over. Sometimes, it can be a pain to tap over to websites from apps. This is even truer when the website has not been designed with app usage in mind. Facebook is a much easier place to get people converting in that way.

- **You can sell things right from Facebook.** They now have a thriving marketplace that is used by millions of people. One of the most unique parts about Facebook is that it has a marketplace where you can sell your products from. That is a fantastic feature!

That is a pretty exhaustive list, but it does not cover nearly half of all of the reasons why Facebook is such a powerful tool.

Now that I have gone over the biggest reasons, I actually want to start out this time by going over the hottest trends we are seeing right now on Facebook. Because the rest of it will be rather technical, I think this is a more digestible way to start you off.

- **Facebook Stories:** Since the inclusion of this feature, there has been more and more usage of it. Everybody is getting into sharing snapshots of their life on their stories. Keeping your story updated here is almost as important as it is on Instagram.

- **AR/Effects:** Did you know that Facebook has launched its own AR program? It is called Facebook Spaces. It works with the Oculus Rift which is a very common AR set-up people have at home. This is a really cool feature that is gaining a lot of traction.

There are also more effects being added to Facebook Stories all the time. These work the same way as the Snapchat filters. They add fun effects that people just cannot get enough of!

- **360 Photos and Videos:** The ability to take 360 angle photos is an incredible thing. This allows for a much more interactive experience where people are able to see an entire view of the surroundings. This is a really cool way to driven engagement and gives people content they can really get in to.

- **Sharing Memes:** Ah, yes, the favorite of the internet. Every platform has a lot of memes, but Facebook, in particular, is a massive factory for them. Memes were born out of Facebook, and the first memes were commonly shared there. Make sure you are taking full advantage of making your own memes and sharing popular ones to gain more traction!

Those are the trends and fads you need to keep an eye on and make sure you are creating content for! Trends come and go, but these will get you started on the right foot. All of them are pretty classic! As you become more immersed in Facebook, you will understand the trends as they come in waves. Just go with the flow and make your content match everybody else's!

The first step, of course, is going to be creating your Facebook page. This can be for a number of things. You will have the option to choose if it is a business page, for a public image; whatever the case may be!

First, you need to know what images need to be created. In order to help you, here are the sizes you need for all of those images:

- **App Images:** 111px by 740x

- **News Feed:** 504px by 1200px

- **Profile Photo:** 320px by 320px

- **Cover Photo:** 720px by 312px

These are what you need in order to get started. Make sure that you size all of your images correctly! This is super important for making sure you look professional.

Once you have your images down, you need to make sure you fill out your "About Me" section. This is one of the biggest selling points since people like to read about the business they are supporting or the people they are following. There is a few components to making a great About Me" section:

- **Tell people what you are all about.** This is the place where you want to make your mission statement incredibly clear. Talk about what the point of your page is and what you are trying to do. Make sure that people feel compelled to follow you because they agree and want the same things.

- **Talk about what inspires you.** Give a nod to your passions. Outline exactly what makes you tick and what you are working toward. You can mention other creators or artists; whatever you want. Just make sure that everybody gets a good idea about what pushes you to keep reading.

- **Make sure people know who you are.** Do not just talk about your professional life or background. Make sure that it is personal and people get a feel for your personality. Authenticity is very much in right now, so you want to be as authentic as possible in this section.

- **Give credit where it is due.** Make sure that you mention other people in your life who have helped. If you are in business, mention people who work behind the scenes! Just ensure that you are being thankful for the people who have made everything possible. People love that!

This is the best recipe to making sure your About Me page is perfectly put and compelling to those who read it. Some people will pay a professional to write this up for them, which could be a good way to go if you are not particularly gifted as a writer.

Linking up your website to Facebook is also crucial. This is possibly the most important part, to be honest. The end result, if you have a website, is to get leads to convert by clicking over and checking it out. It is super easy to do! Facebook has the section for your website clearly labeled when you edit your page.

Now, how about those pesky analytics we keep talking about? I am going to go over those next! The rest of this chapter will be fairly technical and talk a lot about how to set up ads, what Facebook Pixel is all about, and more. I want you to know how to tackle this in a technical way. That is, of course, the only real way to succeed with social media platforms.

First of all, let us get right into the tools that are provided to you by Facebook. There are a number of them, but the ones below are those that will stand out the most.

- **Page Insights:** When you need data on your page and how it is doing, this is where you will go. It will hold all of your analytics and

- **Pages Manager App:** This is where you can change your profile around, set all of your information, and more.

- **Ads Manager:** When you decide to run an ad, this is what you will use to both create it and manage it.

- **Video View:** This is the place where you can view and set up your videos.

- **Different Ad Options:** If you can think it up, Facebook probably has a way to put it into an ad. They also encompass several marketing tactics that have become integrated into the very foundation of their ad services.

That is quite the list and it goes on for much longer! When you are just starting out, these will be the most important factors in your success.

There is a little more to the ads manager that I would like to go over. First, here are some business terms which will help you majorly in navigating the professional world of social media:

- **CPC (Cost-Per-Click):** This is how you determine how successful your ads are, and where you need to put your money. Essentially, it breaks down to how much you are spending for each person to click over to your website. There are other uses for this in different sectors of business, but this is all you need to know for now.

- **CTR (Click-through Rate):** This is, as the name suggests, the rate at which people are clicking through to your website.

- **Facebook Analytics:** Of course, Facebook Analytics is the suite offered to you by Facebook. This is the most important place to go for all of your data to begin creating ads. Facebook will pull from this data to make suggestions for your ad campaigns as you are creating them.

- **Activity Report:** You can find every post you have ever made right back to the beginning with the activity report. This is an important feature, especially for keeping track of analytics.

These are only a few terms that you need to know about. You will find more and more as you dig into the specifics of the business. There is no way around it; you need to become an expert on marketing in order to proceed in your journey to social media success. Most people view Influencers as spoiled, stupid people who are useless for anything beyond taking nice photos.

This could not be further from the truth.

They are savvy business people who have capitalized on this new age advertising that is becoming more and more popular. They are pioneers on the digital front, paving the way for future generations to begin moving their marketing to more lucrative places. The way of TV and radio advertising is moving out of fashion. The internet is the cheapest, and most successful, place to begin marketing yourself or your business.

One part of understanding basic marketing is knowing what Facebook Pixel is. This is one of the most important tools that they offer. However, it is only used by those who have websites.

If you do not have a website, you will not have much use for it. I always suggest building a website as soon as possible in order to maximize your profits as well as your ability to generate passive revenue. You can even host ads or do affiliate marketing in order to further this.

That is not what this book is about, however.

Right now, I just want to focus on getting you to understand Facebook Pixel a bit more. If you do not have a website yet, you will still want to read this part. This is going to further your understanding and set you up for better success in the future.

So, what is Facebook Pixel? And why is it so important? Let me go over exactly how it works, why you need it, and how to use it.

What is Facebook Pixel?

This is a small code that you input into the header of your website. It will track how many people are clicking over from Facebook, which helps you customize your advertising, run retargeting ads, figure out your target audience, and more. It is an invaluable tool that you cannot live without if you have Facebook as well as a website.

The goal of Facebook Pixel is to increase your traffic and better determine how to further your revenue. Here are some of the different ways you can use it:

- *Conversion Tracking*

- *Retargeting Marketing*

- *Lookalike Audiences*

- *Optimizing Ads*

- *More Access to Tools*

These are only a few of the things which Facebook Pixel can help you achieve. I think it is time to move on to how to install it, however, so that you have a better idea of what you are doing.

How to Install and Use Facebook Pixel

1. First, decide what you are tracking. There are 17 actions that Facebook Pixel will track automatically. However, you can actually set your own tracking. They are called "events," but they really just refer to any action taken on your website. I'll go over the standard events after this.

2. Next, you are going to go into your events manager. You'll use the top-left icon, the three lines, and hit "Pixels" once that box is open.

3. From here, Facebook will bring you to a page where you can click a button that says "Create a Pixel."

4. Simply follow the prompts given by Facebook. You will name the Pixel you create and put in your website's URL.

5. You can choose any number of methods to put the Pixel code on your website. You can use an integrated system that works with websites like Google Tag Manager, Shopify, Wix, and more. You can also choose to take the code and put it in the header yourself.

That is the basic how-to on installing Facebook Pixel! The last piece of information I am going to give you is the different events it will automatically track.

- **Purchase:** Of course, this is whenever a person makes a purchase.

- **Lead:** An action is taken by a potential client that shows their potential to buy from you. This is how you identify who your leads are.

- **Complete Registration:** When a person creates an account on your website. This can also refer to registering their e-mail with you, however.

- **Payment Info:** When a customer puts their card information into your system.

- **Cart Additions:** Whenever something is added to a customer's cart.

- **Wishlist Additions:** Whenever something is added to a customer's wishlist.

- **Searching:** Whenever a customer performs a search on your website.

- **Checkout:** This refers to any action taken in regards to checkout. Regardless if they buy something or not. This is a great way to figure out who you should be retargeting ads toward.

Now that we have talked extensively on Facebook Pixel, let us move into the last topic for this chapter: ad campaigns. I want you to have a full understanding of how to set them up, what I mean by retargeting, and why ad campaigns are so important.

- **What Is Retargeting:** Retargeting is the practice of figuring out who has become a warm lead and then targeting ads toward them. This is especially important for those who have added items to their cart or completed registration. Retargeting is setting ads to show up for those people to remind them to continue the process they started.

- **Why are Ads Important:** I do not think this one needs much explanation! Ads are crucial in getting people to know that you are out there. Without ads, you would see a huge decrease in your click-through rate.

These are two crucial things that you need to understand in order to make it on Facebook. Really, it is not just about Facebook as a social media platform. It is about the ability to get traffic moving to other places, such as your other social media profiles. Facebook is fantastic for a lot of stuff, but at the end of the day, to make it as an Influencer, you have to make sure that you are getting people to your other platforms. Having a large following on one platform is great. Real influencers, however, have a following across the board.

Now, it is time to move on to the next giant in the industry, YouTube. This has been a huge point of entertainment for people for many years. It has now turned into an absolute powerhouse of marketing that cannot be ignored. While YouTube may not be for everybody, it is beyond necessary for those who want to be Influencers. Even if you hate being in front of a camera, you have to learn how to be comfortable with it.

More on all of that in the next chapter, however!

Chapter 4: YouTube

Making Video Production and Filming Set-Up Easy

TV? Who watches TV anymore? The answer to that is fewer and fewer people every year. As services like YouTube Red launch, alongside other streaming services, people are less inclined to have a general TV plan. More and more customers are deciding to pay for online services rather than for cable.

There are a few different levels to YouTube now that they have been expanding their services. Here are the subscriptions available:

- **YouTube TV:** While certainly pricey, this is absolutely a popular service that has begun taking off.

- **YouTube Premium:** This monthly subscription gets rid of pesky ads.

So, as you can see, there are a couple of options that consumers have when deciding where they want to put their money. This is a huge industry now, the idea of being able to control exactly what you watch and being able to do so on-demand. Even beyond this, YouTube offers a slew of videos by creators on

76

literally every topic imaginable. There are even creators who do commentary videos. Essentially, all they do is talk about, well, what other creators are doing.

Many YouTubers are now doing news shows dedicated to covering everything from entertainment news to serious international politics. YouTube is a wealth of information, entertainment, guidance, and more. Whenever you want a tutorial, where do you go? The answer is probably YouTube, if not Google. If you want to learn anything then YouTube is a great destination for it.

As you can imagine, I am going to start this off with the list of reasons why YouTube is a powerhouse you need to make a solid home for yourself in.

- **It is an absolute giant among all ages.** There is not an age group that does not use YouTube. It is one of the best ways to make sure you are marketing to an entire group of people. Of course, Facebook is another fantastic way to do so. However, Facebook can be confusing for older generations to use. YouTube has a friendly user interface that acts similarly to TV. It is also easy to click over to new, related videos.

- **It allows for far more personalized content.** Letting people see your face and hear you speak makes you far more "real" to them. Being authentic and making sure people know what you are all about is key to YouTube. Pictures are one thing, but to have a real connection to your audience you must create videos. YouTube is a great way to do that!

- **You can expand your services.** There are several different ways in which to do this. YouTube offers subscriptions for channels now. This means that people can pay a small fee monthly in order to access more content or even specialized content.

- **Have a talent?** Capitalize on it with YouTube. Even if your talent is unrelated to your brand, you can still capitalize on it with YouTube. This is when you want to start brainstorming all of the things you are best at. Making videos on topics you are knowledgeable in is your best bet. People know when you are making things up and do not know what you are talking about.

In essence, stick to what you are best at.

These, again, are only a few reasons out of many. YouTube is, without a doubt, one of the best ways in order to establish a following. It is even easier when you have made a name for yourself on Facebook and Instagram. It can also be a huge confidence booster since most people struggle with the idea of putting themselves out there in such a personal way.

The first thing to do is to get you started on the platform. It is an incredibly easy process that leaves very little to be confused about. One of the best things about YouTube is how easy it is to use!

The first step is to create your account. You can do this in a few different ways. One of the best ways is to attach it to your Google e-mail related to your business. All people who are trying to become Influencers should always have a professional e-mail through which all of their correspondence takes place. This is non-negotiable. Having an unprofessional e-mail will open up a box of trouble when it comes to communicating with companies or other professionals in the field.

Remember, Influencers are not people who just got lucky. They are people who have worked their way into becoming solid professionals through dedication and perseverance.

When you start your account, you want to make sure you have the graphics to load up. This is a crucial step in making sure that you are ready to go. Never leave any images out when you are getting a social media account set up. In fact, the first order of business should be making sure your branding is there and that everything is filled out accordingly.

Here are the sizes for all of the images you will need to make for YouTube:

- **Channel Cover:** 2560px by 1440px

- **Icon:** 200px by 200px

Keep in mind that there are also websites and programs which allow you to create these images. A lot of the time, they are free, too. However, you also have the option, of course, of having a professional create the images. This tends to be the best option if you can afford it. Finding an artist is super easy, and there are a lot of people who charge very reasonable prices. It is worth looking into!

Creating compelling content for YouTube is not necessarily easy. There are a lot of pieces that go into it, and you need to make sure that you are taking it seriously. A recording studio is one of the best ways to do this. Making sure video and audio quality are up to par is incredibly important. You do not want people to click out of your videos because they cannot understand you, or the video quality is so bad, it is not worth watching.

There are a few different ways you can approach this. If you have an iPhone, you should be good to go! They are notoriously great at capturing great video. However, you will still need a microphone. You can invest a little bit of money to get a great one.

Here are some things to think about when setting up your recording studio:

- **Noise Interference:** This is possibly one of the biggest things to consider. You want to make sure you are in an insolated space. Some YouTubers will put up sound foam, which is always a great idea for a recording studio. Closets make a great space to do this in, as you can control the lighting entirely and can insulate the space.

  Keep in mind whether there is construction, as well, and other sources of erratic noise levels. Your closet may not actually be the best choice if there is construction happening on the opposite side of the wall.

- **Lighting Levels:** Alright, in my opinion, this is, absolutely, the most important thing to keep an eye on.

Lighting is key in making sure that your video is watchable. It is also key to making sure that you do not look like a gremlin after uploading it. Lighting is something you should absolutely research into so that you know what will compliment you and make things clear for your viewers.

- **General Aesthetic:** Make sure that everything is branded. If you have a logo, see if you can get it put on a poster to hang up behind you while you film. Make it look cozy, and like it really is just your space where you hang out. You want to be comfortable! Authenticity is the key to YouTube, so you want people to feel like they are just sitting in your room hanging out with you.

I want to go a little bit more into detail on that last bit. The aesthetic is incredibly important, and branding extends even into YouTube videos. You need to keep in mind what your brand and voice are every step of the way. There can be no inconsistencies if you really want to make yourself known.

I have mentioned that there is some equipment you will need, as well as some other tools. I am going to give you a solid list of all of these things below so that you can get started on the right foot.

Tools You Need to Start Filming

- **Microphone:** Audio is key! Having even a mediocre microphone is absolutely necessary for making sure people can understand what you are saying clearly. It makes your voice sound better and helps to cut down on any noise interference that may be happening.

- **Camera:** Again, if you have a phone with a nice camera, you can start there. However, once you start bringing in viewers, you will need to upgrade. There are some great starter cameras by Canon that you can look into. Some places will allow you to rent a nice camera for a day at an affordable price, too.

- **Notecards:** Always make sure you are planning what you are going to say ahead of time. Use a speech outline, and then make notecards based on that outline. Keep them where you can easily reference them. Normally, they are placed behind the camera, so you do not have to look away to view them.

- **Tripod:** Shaking cameras are a huge issue and your arm is going to get awfully tired holding your phone up. Tripods are great because you can adjust them to fit your needs entirely and to get the exact angle that you want.

- **Soundfoam:** This will help block out any outside noise. You can line your door and walls in it where you are recording.

- **Backdrop:** If you do not have a "nice" wall to film in front of, you can always buy a nice backdrop. These can be fairly cheap and allow for the perfect aesthetic without having to have the perfect home.

All of these elements combine into making a fabulous YouTube channel that you can be proud of. Bringing in the viewers depends on having a great aesthetic that pulls people in. They will not watch you if they cannot understand what you are saying, or they think your videos are of poor quality. In the modern age, it is a race to keep up and we need to be the ones at the forefront of that race.

The next thing to think about is your intro and outro. There are several different ways you can tackle this, but you should always have one that is respective to your brand. Many places offer stock videography so that you can make a beautiful intro and outro with the footage you did not take. Getting stock videos is pretty easy, although you do have to pay for them. Adobe offers stock, along with a few other places. You can look around and find the best place for you, although I do always suggest Adobe!

Editing is another huge part. In fact, you will spend far more time editing a video than you will on recording it. This is due to a number of factors, but most of it has to do with the need for post-production fixes. The best programs to use for the job always come on Apple computers. In fact, if you are going to become a social media guru and Influencer, you need to invest in Apple gear. While there is a lot of contention about how pricey they are compared to how much they offer, they really are industry standard. All of the video editing software you could ever need is right there on a Mac.

There are a few best practices I am going to go over before I talk about some of the trends to watch out for. These next two sections will conclude this chapter!

Video sizing is important, and you need to understand how large the video you are recording should be. Here are some of the dimensions that you are going to need to know:

- **YouTube Video Size:** 1920px x 1080px

- **Standard Resolution:** 1080p

- **Thumbnail Sizing:** 1280px by 720px

You may prefer a different size. This would be largely dependent on how you plan on using YouTube. However, that is going to be further down the line once you really begin to understand what you are doing. This book is just the first, big step to doing that!

The next thing you need to know is how to select a great thumbnail. This is what people will see as the "preview" of your video. It is crucial that you make sure you pick a good one and keep them consistent. The thumbnail is the first impression that a potential lead gets, so you need to make sure it interests them enough to make them click on it. Those conversions are important no matter where you are on the internet!

How to Select a YouTube Video Thumbnail

1. Go to the YouTube Studio app. You can then go tap the menu button.

2. Once in the menu, you are going to tap "Videos."

3. Look for the video which you are trying to add your thumbnail to. Once you find it, select the "edit" option provided. You will then be prompted to click Edit Thumbnail next.

4. Go to "Custom Thumbnail." It is from here that you will be able to upload a custom image you have made for that video.

They also provide a selection of thumbnails that are automatically generated by YouTube. However, these are not what you want to go with. Remember: you must stay consistently branded right down to the thumbnail selection on your videos.

Now that you know how to select the thumbnail, let us talk a little bit more about how to create the perfect one for your video and brand. Here are the best tips I have in order to make sure you have a thumbnail that will pull your cold leads right in:

Tips for Creating a Great Thumbnail

- **Always make sure you are using the most optimized sizing.** If a photo is not an ideal size, it will come out blurry and distorted. This is part of the reason that getting Photoshop is so necessary to your success. When it comes to editing thumbnails, this program is your best bet to get the best result.

- **Choose an edited photo that matches your brand.** Again, it is all about that consistency. You can edit your photo with the same filters or affects you use for the others.

- **Make sure you add text that pulls people in.** Use a big, bold title that tells people what the video is all about. Or, use words like "Wow!" You can scroll through YouTube and check out other thumbnails to figure out the best words to put down and what is working for other YouTubers. Remember, market research is also crucial!

- **Use a legible font that is preferable to the font you use for your whole brand.** You will need to buy a font at some point, but buying a license for them tends to be fairly cheap until you are looking to sell merchandise with that font.

- **Make sure that you are using complementary, bold colors.** You want that thumbnail to pop out and catch the person's attention. Make sure that the colors you use do not clash and that they blend together nicely. However, you want some great contrast so that people can actually see what they are looking at and tell it all apart.

Finally, let me go over some hot trends that are happening. I am going to also list out some cool challenges that YouTubers are taking part in. You want to make sure that you are keeping up with what is hot and what is pulling in views. Getting on board with trends is a great way to show your audience that you are fun and love to do silly things for the camera. These video trends are also a great way to create content without having to come up with the idea and flesh it out yourself.

The Hottest Trends on YouTube Right Now

- **Shopping Videos:** People love shopping. There is something about spending money that is ultimately satisfying to us. It gets dopamine and serotonin flowing, and there are plenty of studies showing the pleasure centers which are activated because of shopping.

  For this reason, a lot of YouTubers are doing "immersive shopping" where they bring you shopping with them. Another way to do this is to do "haul" videos where you show everything that you bought at the store and, normally, the prices of those items.

- **Gift Guides:** When the holidays approach, it is time to think about gifts. There is no better way to start pulling in views than jumping on the gift guide bandwagon. No matter what kind of channel you are, you can do this. Gift guides are necessary for all types of people, so capitalize on this free content idea that is so incredibly popular.

- **Daily Routines:** People love watching others who seem to have their life together. This is a way to live vicariously through others and to perhaps inspire you to do better in your   own   life.

Putting together a daily routine video is normally not about putting together your "real" daily routine. You want to keep it authentic, sure, but make it the routine of your ideal day. The point is for people to guilt themselves into doing better; we all do it!

- **What I Eat in a Day:** Another one that has been gaining a lot of traction is letting people see what you eat in a day. This is an offshoot of the "mukbang" trend that has been losing popularity as of late. This is especially popular for those people who may have a specialized diet or specific dietary needs. It also works well for lifestyle bloggers, foodies (of course), and fitness coaches.

This is where I leave when you when it comes to YouTube. I think that the hottest trends will get you started in the right direction, as will the other information I have provided on this page. Make sure to reference the image sizing and other things you need by adding a bookmark to those pages.

Next comes another giant on the scene right now. While at first a lot of people did not really take to it, this company has seen explosive growth in popularity. We all know what that little blue bird represents! That is right: I am talking about Twitter. I cannot wait to teach you how to successfully use the ultimate source for information sharing!

Chapter 5: Twitter

How to Tweet Your Way to an Influencer Status

That blue bird has become crucial to the younger generation. It allows for rapid-fire information sharing and a way to stay constantly updated.

However, the downside of Twitter is that it can be immensely confusing at first. This chapter will err on the longer side because of this fact. Twitter is arguably one of the easier platforms to grow on, but that happens once you understand what is going on. However, that is, of course, where I come in.

There are many different reasons for you to jump on the Twitter train. Let me go over some below so that you can have a better understanding of why it is so crucial to your business:

- **It forces people to be concise and get their point across.** Because of the 140-character limit, everybody needs to boil their thoughts down. This is great because a lot of people do not want to read paragraphs of text. People are more likely to read your tweets because they know that it is all they are going to have to read.

- **You can easily monitor your competitors.** The consistent stream of tweets most brands put out means you can keep track of what they are up to. Many of them use Twitter to announce releases and encourage hype for their products. It also helps you see who is choosing to go with them and give you a new idea for a target audience for ads.

- **Information is shared consistently and constantly.** Twitter is the best at encouraging constant interaction. People are often scrolling through their feed because of the consistent interactions provided. Engagement is through the roof if you do Twitter correctly.

- **Engagement with others is the entire point.** As mentioned above, Twitter is great for driving engagement. The entire purpose of the platform is to interact with others. Twitter's simplicity is the very reason for its popularity. There is really no point to Twitter except for putting your thoughts out there, and also responding to the thoughts of others.

Again, there are far more reasons, but these are the biggest ones that come to mind. Twitter is undoubtedly wildly popular, and it is not going anywhere anytime soon. Once Instagram is established and doing well, I always suggest moving to Twitter next. This is the next step in putting your brand on the map.

Let's get over the image sizes for Twitter, and the best way to make your photos. I also will go over the best schedule for this social media platform. Twitter is one of those apps where you are really going to want to start scheduling posts ahead of time. This allows you to check-in spontaneously but still know that you are putting out content consistently.

Image Sizes for Twitter

- **Header:** 1500px by 500px

- **Icon:** 400px by 400px

- **Posts:** 600px by 335px

You really need to make sure that you are optimizing these images. It is important to do so for every single platform you are part of. Twitter is especially important because the images are so finicky. There is a limited amount of "safe space" in posts. This means that the image will be "cut off" until you tap on it to expand it. You must make sure the text is centered perfectly to take care of this problem.

Making great images is a snap with the programs I provided earlier. You can also find places online that will help you make sure your photos are optimized for Twitter. This is the most important step.

Growing your Twitter is probably the topic you are most interested in reading about. So, let us get right into that portion of this chapter! Here are the best ways you can start to grow your following:

- **Respond to Others:** The best way to get your name out there is to always respond to people. The sooner you do so, the better. It is easy to start dialogues on Twitter and exchange witty .GIFs and snippets. This increases your chance of somebody following you, especially if they like the aesthetic of your brand.

- **Hold Mini-Contests:** Remember back earlier in the book when I wrote out some terms for you? Call to action was one of them. Holding mini-contests is a great way to put that marketing principle into play. You simply put a prompt of some sort in your profile. It could be to give a caption to a photo, or some other silly, fun theme.

  Ask people to retweet and comment. Offer to follow everybody who interacts. One of the best ways to get higher engagement on Twitter is making sure that you are offering to follow those who engage with you. You do not have to follow people back if they follow you. There is a lot of culture surrounding this, and some people may unfollow if you do not follow back. However, at the end of the day, it is not a rule set in stone.

I recommend following back on Twitter until you hit about 600 followers.

- **Participate in Follow Friday:** One of the best ways, in order to ensure you are driving engagement, is to do "Follow Fridays." This is when people Tweet to their respective "communities" a specific hashtag with the offer of following the person back. The Tweet normally looks something like this:

"Hey, #fitnesscommunity! I'm starting a #FollowFriday train! Leave me a .gif telling me about your day, and I will follow you!"

Again, this is a great way to perform a call to action. You are asking them to do something fun, and in exchange, you're going to follow them. That is a fairly low risk, high reward situation. It is because of this that people are more likely to comment. You may be able to get as many as 50 followers during a Follow Friday. It is an excellent strategy.

Make sure to add in emojis to spice things up a little bit. Of course, you may have a different target market than the fitness community. You will figure out with time which hashtags are best suited to whatever market you are in. This comes with time taken in doing research into the market. On Twitter, field research is best.

You should also tag some people if you have room to. When you tag people, the Tweet will look like this:

"Hey, #fitnesscommunity! How about a #followfriday? RT or comment and I will follow you! Here are some people you should follow: @fitnessperson1, @fitnessperson2, @fitnessperson3..."

Of course, you will insert the names of people. It does not matter if you talk to them or not. If they are following you, or you are following them, feel free to tag them. This is what gets your name out there. You just need to figure out how you are going to attack it because you only have 140 characters to do it in!

- **Keep Up with Trending Hashtags:** Speaking of hashtags and field research, I think it is time to bring up the issue of hashtags. While there are other platforms where they are somewhat ineffective, Twitter remains solidly attached to hashtags. This is the best way in order to get your Tweet seen by others, right alongside directly tagging people in your Tweets.

There are a few different ways in order to figure out which hashtags are best. I am going to go over that after I complete this list. I want to make sure you have the tools you need in order to put your Tweet onto the front page of every lead's feed!

- **Post at the Right Times:** The best way to figure out when you should post is via a program like HootSuite. In fact, HootSuite was actually created originally for managing Twitter accounts. It has specialized tools to run all aspects of your social media, but Twitter especially benefits from it being integrated into your social media plans.

Figuring out when you can expect periods of high-volume traffic allows you to reach as many people as possible. Again, social media is free to use, if you do not have all the bells and whistles. This is why making sure you understand your analytics and know where to access them is so important. The more you know about how to make those numbers work for you, the less money you will have to spend in the long run. It really is about using your   resources.

HootSuite will find the best times and schedule your tweets accordingly. Just make sure if you are doing "themed" tweets, which I will be going over down below, that they all match up accordingly and are in the correct order.

- **Participate in Themes:** Are the holidays around the corner? Is it almost Thanksgiving? Is Father's Day approaching? No matter what holiday is on the horizon, there is going to be a chance to churn out the content accordingly. You should expect to begin planning for the holiday season well in advance. From October to April, your social media calendar should be jampacked with fun,   holiday-related   tweets.

The best part? These are all free content ideas. You just ask questions related to the holiday, especially as it relates to your niche. So, if you were a part of the writing community, you could ask people what books they want for presents. Fitness community? Ask for stories about how their parents inspired their fitness journeys near Mother's or Father's day.

Make sure to keep in the back of your mind when your company or brand was founded. You should always make a "1-year" post to celebrate, and perhaps a giveaway, as well.

- **Host Giveaways:** This is probably one of the best ways to get your account to grow, grow, grow. People love free things, and you can put together a lovely giveaway for a pretty low price. This is even truer when you team up with other brands in order to make the giveaway happen. By now, if you are following my steps, you should have a successful Instagram account. Try and contact brands you have hosted giveaways with before and see if they would like to do one with you on Twitter.

You can also use this to drive people from one platform to the other. Post on your Instagram, Facebook, and other social media accounts. Tell people about the giveaway that is happening on Twitter and give them a link to follow you. This will encourage people to follow you on multiple platforms, making it more likely that they will follow you on the rest.

There are a few steps for giveaways that I will also list after the rest of these items on the list. I will put it below how to find the best hashtags so that you can figure out how to do both easily.

These tweets drive major engagement because to enter, there are some rules. Normally, you will have them retweet it once a day and tag some friends in the comments. More on that below!

- **Don't Be Afraid to Follow:** I always suggest keeping a low follow-to-follower ratio. On Instagram, this matters a lot. However, on Twitter, it matters far less. You still want to keep that ratio low for brand prestige. However, you can let it go for far longer. While I said 600 followers should be the cut-off above, for some industries, you may need to go upwards of 2-3k. You will figure out how to balance it all out once you begin to work more on Twitter.

In the beginning, follow anybody who interacts with your posts. When you do Follow Fridays, you can tag people you are following to get them to interact. Keep in mind that you can unfollow people. Some say it is rude, but there is no point in following 5k+ people. At that point, there is no way to bond and really get to know the people you are following.

Those who you choose to follow should always be people you aspire to be like. They should be professionals in the industry, big influencers within your niche, companies you want to work with, or anything else along those lines. Unfollow people who have poor-quality content or who you do not see yourself forming a business relationship with further on.

It is all about quality control.

- **Be Consistent with Content:** Again, I really do suggest using a scheduling platform for Twitter. Using HootSuite or Buffer will free up quite a bit of your time. In fact, they are pretty much indispensable for this platform. It is really hard to get out consistent content to Twitter that is branded and high-quality on the fly. It is better to sit down and brainstorm exactly how you want things to go and when you should be Tweeting what.

This is even truer because of the fact that there are so many themed days and other activities on Twitter. I will have more below on how to make the best social media calendar for Twitter especially, and what graphics you should make to go along with them.

- **Use Your Other Platforms:** By now, you should have at least a couple of other platforms. Facebook is good to just have on the backburner regardless of whether you use it, and Instagram should be your go-to first choice. If you do not yet have a website, a great way to link people is to put your Twitter URL in the "website" box.

  This will put an active link to it on your account regardless of whether or not you have the ability to have people swipe-up to links yet (this is given at 10k followers if you do not remember me mentioning it in the Instagram   chapter).

  For Facebook, you can do the same thing. You can also easily make a post about it, and also link it in the "About Us" or "Mission Statement." In fact, I encourage you to cross-link as much as possible. For Twitter, this is especially important because it allows followers to get to know you better. Twitter is where you will really make them fall in love with your brand and what you are all about.

These are the best ways in which to begin growing your Twitter account. There are a couple of more things I want to go over in relation to growing an account before I get into some hot trends.

As I said, this is a fairly long chapter. However, I think that you will be incredibly ready to take Twitter by storm after you are done reading it. I want you to be as confident as possible because I recognize that Twitter is one of the hardest platforms to "get."

Of course, you will "get" it in full after you are done reading this chapter.

How to Find the Best Hashtags

First, you are going to do some market research. I am going to do this from the perspective of somebody who is running a fitness blog. It is the idea that you need to follow, not the specific hashtags I am going to mention. Just tweak it to fit whichever niche you happen to fall into.

- **First, go into the search bar on Twitter.** From here, you are going to put in the search term "Fitness" and go to that hashtag. This is a great place to start for following others.

- **Make sure that you set it to post "newest" first, not "trending."** You want to respond to people who have just posted and putting the newest first allows you to do so.

- **I will normally scroll back for about ten minutes.** During this, I will be reacting to, commenting on, and re-tweeting things as I scroll down. These will be people who have very recently been on Twitter. Chances are they will still be lurking around and will respond almost instantly to you. Interaction is always key!

- **As you are scrolling down, take note of all the different hashtags.** You will begin to notice patterns taking hold, and this will clue you in to which hashtags are trending in that specific niche.

- **Compile your three different groups of hashtags I talked about earlier.** You will want three groups of entirely different hashtags that you will cycle through at random. This will give you the highest chance of being seen by different accounts across the board.

- **Repeat this market research daily.** You do not have to compile your lists of hashtags daily. That will be done in one go the first time you scroll through and do this. You may update those lists as tie goes on, however, and that   is   a   good   idea,   too.

Instead, you just want to repeat scrolling down, looking at hashtags, checking trends, and interacting with others.

Ten minutes a day is really all it takes, along with your scheduled Tweets, to get the ball rolling.

How to Host a Great Giveaway

Giveaways can be a double-edged sword. On the one hand, people love getting free stuff. On the other hand, they can be a hassle to deal with and can land you in hot water if they are not done correctly. There are certain rules and regulations which fall into play when it comes to hosting a giveaway. Let me lay out the steps, and rules you should put into place, below.

- **Decide on the theme of the giveaway.** The first step, of course, is figuring out what theme you want the giveaway to have. A good plan is to wait until you have 1,000 followers and throw a giveaway in celebration of this. It depends on how fast you grow and how quickly you would like to invest money into your Twitter, however.

For fitness bloggers, you could do a butt boosting workout kit. If you doing food blogging, you could do a giveaway for a set of great kitchen tools or even a gift card. Sometimes, theming it with holidays or other events can be cool. Self-care is a great theme to go with during the holidays, for example, because of stress induced by the   season.

Just think about it for a while and you will come up with some great ideas!

- **Ask others to co-host with you.** This is one of the best ways to drive costs down. However, it really does hinge on you having the correct following. You can ask companies to partner with you, but this means you need to already have a status as a micro-influencer to convince them.

  Otherwise, you can ask other accounts, perhaps with a larger following, to team up with you. If you provide the goodies for the giveaway, microinfluencers are normally open to partners for free.

- **Figure out who is doing what.** When you decide to bring co-hosts into the mix, there needs to be responsibility delegated. This is only true if you are doing so with other accounts similar to yours, however. Influencers and micro-influencers will expect you to do everything   except   for   promotion.

  Keeping spreadsheets is a great way to keep track of

everything. Google Drive is an industry-standard. I already mentioned this, but it bears repeating. Make sure that you know how to use it and that this is where you keep the majority of your documents.

- **Begin planning and scheduling posts.** You will want to do this long before the giveaway is announced. Figure out day-by-day what you are going to need to be posted in regard to it. Make all of the photos ahead of time and carefully plan them in a strategic fashion. If you are using HootSuite, you can have it figure out the best times to post for you.

- **Order the goodies and take photos.** Once you have everything ordered, you need to take photos. This is where the multiple different platforms start to teach you the knowledge that you need. Photography is essential to your everyday life as an influencer or somebody looking to expand their company in a digital space.

Make sure the giveaway items are clear and crisp, and that they are arranged in an aesthetically pleasing way. You can look at flat lay inspirations to find better ideas of how to arrange things.

- **Do a "Live" broadcast.** This is a great way to generate hype. You can schedule in posts which count down to the live event where you will announce the giveaway, talk about how to join, and show off what is included in the giveaway. This is optional, however, depending on your schedule and how much effort you can put into that particular   campaign.

The best part about Twitter, after all, is being able to load up posts and only check in once a day to respond to things. Do not push yourself more than you have to.

- **Lay out rules which are meant to drive engagement.** There are some rules you need to make sure you get right. You only have 140 characters to hook people,   after   all.

I recommend creating a graphic you will attach to the post. Lay out the rules clearly on this graphic in a great, bold font. This will let you hook people with the actual tweet, and not take up any space with rules you could use for   hashtags   and   the   hook.

Here   are   the   rules   which   I   suggest:
You   must   retweet   this   once   a   day
You   must   tag   three   friends   in   the   comments
You must leave a comment telling a story about time fitness   helped   you   get   through   a   rough   patch

The last one will obviously be changed, again, to fit your niche. The point is that you want people to tag others, exponentially extending your reach, and to also retweet daily. Both of these things will give you a far greater ability to find leads and attract them in.

Asking them to tell a story, or comment anything else, is a call to action, as well. You are asking them to engage more actively with you.

- **Keep track of entries intelligently.** Create a system on keeping track of the entries. You need to make sure you do this correctly and everybody actually gets a fair shot. You can always, of course, decide on a random winner yourself. Some people do this because it can take a lot of time to actually track entries. However, that is up to your own moral breakdown.

- **Make sure to figure out how you are deciding on winners.** Most people will use a random generator. If the giveaway is small enough, you could even write them all down on pieces of paper and actually draw their name out on video. You can tackle it however you would like, but make sure that you celebrate by posting all about it and congratulating the winner. This is the last push for hype you will get out of this.

You should put a little, handwritten card in the giveaway, too. Write something nice and thank them for participating. It is the little things that go a long way in winning over your followers.

How to Create a Social Media Calendar

I have spoken quite extensively on how important a social media calendar is to those who are using social media professionally. HootSuite will give you the option to make one on their website, as will Buffer. However, you should also be fully capable of making one yourself. In order to help you do this, I am going to lay out how to schedule posts for Twitter. I recommend especially to schedule things for Twitter since it is an extremely "low maintenance" platform when you do so.

- **Pick how you are going to track it.** Some people prefer a digital method of tracking their daily tasks. There are countless apps, websites, and programs that offer to-do lists and other ways to manage your life. Others may prefer keeping track on a physical medium, such as a wall calendar. Whatever you do, make sure that it is big enough to hold all of the information you need.

If you are going with a physical calendar, I suggest picking up the following supplies to help you:

Sticky *notes*
Highlighters
White-Out
Sharpies
Stickers

All of these will help you color code and better define the calendar. The point is to know what is happening at a glance. You will figure out how to stay more and more organized as you go along, however.

- **Create a different calendar for each platform.** Do not attempt to schedule all platforms with one calendar. This is a rookie mistake. You are going to need all of them, preferably color-coded. Keeping your different platforms separated is key in keeping things organized and knowing what is happening. Besides, you cannot schedule the same post for multiple accounts. Things need to be optimized for the platform on which you are posting.

- **Make sure you create a list of what you will need.** Take some time to brainstorm about how you will be keeping track of things. While Buffer and HootSuite are great, you need to have a calendar that keeps track of things for the entirety of the campaign you are planning. It is best to use something that is separate you have to write in specifically. Writing things down helps you commit them to memory and helps you see flaws in your own   plans.

Consistency is key, but organization is even more important.

- **Keep track of your ideas for asking questions.** You will find that you think of questions to ask people in your posts as you are just going about your day-to-day life. Do not be afraid to keep a notepad on you and write them down as they come. It is kind of like being a writer. Eventually, you will just start brainstorming all the time.

Tweets, where you ask a question, are incredibly popular and great at driving that high engagement you want.

- **Study your analytics so you know when to post.** I know this is basically beating a dead horse at this point. However, analytics are the bread and butter of anybody who is looking to make money on social media. There are a number of ways I have already gone over through which you can check your analytics. You have the tools, just make sure you are using them.

- **Make sure all settings on HootSuite or Buffer are ready to go.** You will want to check over all of the settings, including the time zone they are being posted in. Make sure to use your own time zone and to base all of the times off of this. The internet is a global network, so it is important to let people know specifically when something is going to end based on your time zone. You do not want to promise results at 8 am and not have them post until 3 pm because of a mess up with your settings.

- **Schedule things accordingly.** Make sure that you put everything in order. Take care to name files correctly. This relates to organizing things, but it is more specific than that. Be careful and look through to make sure you are scheduling the right posts with the right bits of text. You can drag and drop any that need to be switched around. Luckily, all of that is pretty easy to do.

- **Wait and watch!** Now, all that is left to do is sit back, relax, and engage once the likes, comments, and retweets start rolling in. This will allow you to mostly ignore Twitter while you still have a low number of followers and low engagement but builds up engagement slowly since you are constantly churning out content.

Those are the best tips and tricks I can give you for staying afloat in the wild world that is Twitter. I know that it is a lot less scary now. To round off this chapter, I will go over the hottest ways to stay current with the current generation. Twitter is the hottest among the youth, with almost every teenager actively on it. This shows in its exploding popularity and growing relevance.

Here are the hottest trends you need to engage with:

- **This or That:** You can play this using the "poll" feature. It is a great way to get people interacting since we love to tap a button and get instant gratification from it. We can see the answer and know whether we have the "correct" opinion or not. It is addictive and totally taking off.

  To play "This or That," simply tweet a poll asking whether your followers prefer one thing or another. You should add some emojis and hashtags in the text to catch their attention. Not too many, but perhaps, a couple of relevant ones. You can also ask them to respond with a .gif of their favorite!

Here are some popular ones:

Cake	*or*	*Pie*
Camping	*or*	*Clubbing*
Ocean	*or*	*Lake*
Tea	*or*	*Coffee*
Morning *Person*	*or*	*Night* *Owl*

You can use your imagination to come up with more. It is even better when you really customize it in order to fit into your niche. So, again, if you are a fitness blogger, you ask "Push-Ups or Crunches" as your poll.

- **.Gif Responses:** This is when you ask your followers to post a .gif in response to your tweet. Here is an example of what one such tweet might look like:

"Good morning, #fitnesscommunity! Rise and shine! Let me know how you're feeling this morning by responding with a .gif! I'll start!"

Of course, you will add some hashtags and a couple of emojis. Then, attach a .gif to the tweet using the option they provide. Make it a response to whatever question you posed, and then send it out.

- **Follow Trains:** This is similar to a "Follow Friday," but it can be done any day of the week. Follow trains are a great way to build a following and also get introduced to the community. The point at first is to follow anybody and everybody so you can get a good handle on the community at large. Again, you will eventually want to stop and begin to cull out accounts you do not like, but at first, you need to know what is up.

  To create a follow train, write a tweet saying you are starting one and use the hashtag #followtrain. Make sure to add hashtags that are community- and niche-specific.

- **Tweeting Games:** These are a fantastic way to get people interacting with you. They also, however, get them to interact with each other. This is great as it drives engagement, in the end, to you. Playing little games in the comments is fun, lighthearted, and can produce hilarious results. This is a great way to bond with your followers!

That last entry is an important one. Many of you will probably not know what a "tweeting game" is. Because of this, I am going to give you a few games you can play with your followers on Twitter. You can use these when you are first beginning to schedule content to post onto Twitter. Just follow the directions for the game, tweak it to match your brand and niche, and you will have great content ready to go.

3 Tweeting Games to Play

- **Respond to the Person Above You:** In this game, you will tweet that each person should respond to the person above them with a .gif. You will start by attaching your own .gif. You can do this as a theme to days or in any capacity you would like. You may want to wait until you have a higher volume of followers beforehand, however. Having friends who will join in is a bonus. Once people start going in, it has a kind of snowball effect!

- **Make a Wish, Ruin a Wish:** In this game, you make a wish. The next person responds granting you the wish... but with a shocking, horrible, but hilarious, twist. They then make a wish, and the person who responds to them does the same. It has a ripple effect and can have hilarious results... especially when peppered with .gifs!

- **Write a Story:** You will tweet out five words to begin a story. Normally, you will tailor this to fit your niche. You will then invite people to add to the story by RTing it, adding a line at a time. This can also have some surprising results, especially as more people begin to join in with it.

I hope that you have some ideas for content now. If you rotate through those and do one every other day, you should have quite a bit of content stocked up alongside the other ideas I have given you. Twitter can be perplexing to those unfamiliar with it. It is entirely separate from the other social media giants and absolutely presents its own challenges. However, once you begin to develop an understanding of it, everything starts to make sense.

Twitter is not necessarily hard to learn. It is just largely unfamiliar. After reading this chapter, I hope that it feels a little less alien next time you go onto your account. Just keep doing what I told you to do earlier. Spend ten minutes scrolling through the new posts on a few big tags, interact, and keep your Buffer or HootSuite queue stocked up!

Now that we have gone over the major social media platforms for the public, I think it is time to round this book out with a chapter specifically made for aspiring professionals. This next topic is for the "Facebook of Professionals," as some people have deemed it. People are flocking more and more to this space in order to develop themselves, look into employers, and find relevant, meaningful jobs.

LinkedIn is, without a doubt, a necessary tool for all of those seeking work in a professional field. This next chapter is going to cover everything you need to know about this platform you may have never even heard of.

Chapter 6: LinkedIn

The Facebook of Professionals Made Easy for Blooming Business Minds

First of all, you are probably wondering what LinkedIn even is. Some call it the "Facebook of Professionals." I suppose you could call it that, to an extent, but there is far more to LinkedIn than meets the eye. You cannot simply identify it in such a way because of the fact that there is so much that goes into it.

In this day and age, we can stay in touch no matter what. At the tap of a screen, we are in contact with whoever we want in an instant. This ability to network at such a quick pace is greatly impacting the search for jobs. It can make it easier, or more difficult, depending on quite a few circumstances. There are many remote jobs popping up because of the internet, which is helpful to many. However, with such a quick-paced modern interview process, jobs are snatched up before you even get your chance.

LinkedIn steps in to offer the boost that any aspiring professional could need. There are quite a few functions that it serves, all of which I will go over. For now, let me get into why exactly you should be using LinkedIn. I think it will help better explain what this social networking platform is all about. First, I am going to go over why influencers specifically should look into it.

After this, I will make an entry specifically related to businesses. Since those are the two groups most likely to be reading this, I think I should highlight the major differences so that you can take the best path for yourself.

Why Should Influencers Use LinkedIn?

- **This is a great place to network with sponsors.** Not only are you interacting on other forms of social media, but you are now interacting with them in a professional capacity. This certainly gets more attention and is taken more seriously.

  It is easier to get sponsors to come to you when they see that you are worth the money spent on advertising. Being able to link potential sponsors to your LinkedIn is never a bad touch, either. It is a true seal of legitimacy.

- **You can easily put your numbers at a glance.** There are a lot of statistics and numbers which go along with analytics. That is the nature of the beast when it comes to social media marketing. LinkedIn allows you to put all of this information there for people to see.

You can proudly display your achievements as it relates to follower count, engagement rates, and the rest. This will be part of your influencer resume, but it never hurts to put the information on the profile as well as in the attachment.

- It is easy to prove yourself to companies when your skills are verified. This is something that will come up, and be explained more, below. For now, just know that having verified skills is a huge thing on LinkedIn. The more verified you are, and the bigger your network, the better.

- **Looking for a job in social media is far easier.** Many people who go the influencing route take jobs handling social media for companies. This presents a fantastic opportunity for you to do what you love and make good money at it.

Some influencers are able to work part-time for a company and survive for the rest of it on their ad revenue and sponsorships. Trying to live off of your social media as much as possible is the name of the game! However, in the meantime, LinkedIn is the place to go when you want a legitimate job in the industry.

There are other places, sure, but the best part about LinkedIn is how legitimate everything is. You can view networks, see verifications, and really vet companies before you agree to work with them.

- **You have a home for all three of your resumes.** Did you hear that right? Three resumes? Unfortunately, this is the truth. Influencers should actually have three resumes to show: a marketing portfolio, an influencer resume, and a standard resume. While one of those is technically a portfolio, it really is just a glorified list of what you have done so far. I will go into the differences, and what an Influencer resume is, after this next section.

Why Should Businesses Use LinkedIn?

- **It is insanely easy to hire people.** LinkedIn is a hotspot for budding professionals and seasoned veterans alike. When you need to hire somebody, going through LinkedIn can garner some amazing results. The website goes above and beyond to make sure they are fitting together employers with candidates that really fit.

  If you need employees, you want this to be the main source you pull from.

- **Monitor what your competition is doing.** Of course, keeping an eye on what your competition is doing never hurts. This gives you a chance to not only check out their company's LinkedIn page but to also network with some of the professionals at that company.

  I am not talking about trading insider info, of course. I am just suggesting that broadening your network is never a bad thing, especially in an industry where who you know is everything.

- **Build a more trustworthy brand.** Because LinkedIn is considered the best place for professionals on the internet, it is a great place to help legitimize your brand. Your business looks so much better when a LinkedIn page pops up with links to your amazing profile and the amazing profiles of any employees you bring on!

- **Network with people you want to work with.** Just like with influencers looking for sponsors, LinkedIn is also a great place for sponsors looking for influencers. You can easily vet candidates and check out their stats and resumes before you reach out to them. This is a powerful tool in hand-selecting who you think would be the best.

- **Have a "breathing" resume for yourself.** Since you most likely do not have a "resume" anymore, as you won your own business, this is a way to keep the information alive. Your LinkedIn profile is, essentially, an incredibly intricate resume through which employers can see your expertise. It also helps that there is a way that others can verify your skills and leave recommendations. I will get into both of those later, however!

No matter what happens, if you have a LinkedIn, you will have something to show in case your business fails. This is absolutely a worst-case scenario but, all things considered, businesses really do fail all of the time. The key is persistence and perseverance. Just because you have to go back to work for a while and put your business on the back burner does not make you less of a businessperson.

These are a few of the major reasons why both Influencers and business owners should be on LinkedIn. There are many more, but you will begin to understand that as this chapter continues on. LinkedIn has a lot to offer to everybody, and there are several different features it has. Most people prefer it to Facebook because it is filled with motivational posts, business-related blogs, and news articles that you do not want to miss.

However, because of how niche it is, LinkedIn can be confusing. This is even worse for those who may never have worked in a professional capacity before. Unfortunately, there is no quick fix. You simply have to get on the platform and begin playing around with it. Once you are done reading this, you should have the info you need to build your account from the ground up. Do not worry too much about it. For now, keep reading and know that this is invaluable information that will take you to success!

LinkedIn is easy enough to create a go-to place to see what your brand is officially spreading. If you are an Influencer, use it as a chance to talk about social media, the industry you work in, and more. Flex your skills in marketing and show the professional world that you are a true player among them. Remember, Influencers are truly savvy businesspeople who know what they are doing. You want to make sure that you are exactly that. LinkedIn can help you get there.

It is okay if you do not post anything at first. In fact, I recommend that you wait at least a couple of months. I know that sounds like a super long time, but the reality is that LinkedIn is not like the other platforms. Anything you put on it will be scrutinized and shown to reflect you in the professional world. This is, arguably, a much smaller pond than the others.

I recommend perusing articles, sharing ones you agree with, and really building your skill base and knowledge. Once you have great analytics to show for it, and you have built yourself a following, you can begin to figure out what articles you would be best to write for.

There are a few functions you should know about when you first get on.

Once you have successfully set up your profile, you need to begin networking with people. There are a few ways you can begin to reach out to those in your network. These will only work if you have had professional experience with them.

Look for those who you have worked with, or for, and then look for employees of yours. Even clients count! Here are the two best ways to show appreciation to your network and get a little appreciation back:

- **Verify Their Skills:** In order to do this, you will scroll down to the "Skills" section. It is large, and you really cannot miss it. The user interface of LinkedIn is pretty friendly! It will give you the choice to verify the skill. Going through and doing this for all the skills you know about is the best way to encourage them to do the same for you.

- **Leave Them a Review:** If you have worked with the person, you may want to leave them a review. You can say something nice about them and mention how great they were to work with. This is a nice touch that everybody appreciates.

Both of these will help others you know. It is common courtesy to return the favor, so you should see others begin to do the same for you. This step is important because it allows you to begin solidifying your now completed profile. Keep in mind, however, that you should not leave reviews for those you do not know very well. You should also avoid verifying skills you do not actually see in action. This kind of dishonest reviewing is wrong, and it is also kind of tacky. People do not like dishonesty as a rule in the professional world even when that dishonesty is benefiting them.

Now, I want to walk you through exactly how to set your profile up. I am going to give you the dimensions for the photos first, of course. After this, however, I am going to talk about what you should choose as your photos. This is not your social media account; this is your professional presence on a networking platform. There are some rules and general guidelines you should be going by.

- **Profile Photo:** This should be a headshot of you, preferably. You want it to be high-res and highly professional looking. Depending on what you are using LinkedIn for, you can add a personal flare. If you are a fitness influencer, for example, you may post a high-quality photo of you working out. It should, of course, look   clean   and   be   presentable.

Remember that the profile photo is going to represent everything you are to the people looking at it. We make judgments in microseconds about others. LinkedIn is all about the presence and the image you portray. Reflect that you understand this by literally portraying the right images.

Recommended Size: 400px by 400px

- **Cover Photo:** Your cover photo is a little more tricky. This should be more personalized to you and should better show your personality. If you like to ride horses in your spare time, put a pretty picture of you riding. If you are a food blogger, post a photo of you in your element making   food.

Just make sure that this is also a high-quality, professional photo. That is the key here. I am not going to keep repeating it. I think you get the point.

Recommended Size: 1536px by 768px

I always recommend hiring a professional to do your photos. Once you start becoming a microinfluencer, you will need to become good at photography, too. You can always do your own headshots and photos if you find you have a talent for it. However, many influencers will still hire people to do this for them. It depends on how comfortable you are with it and whether you think you need a professional hand for the job.

The next bit you need to think about is your resume. Like I mentioned previously, there are normally three you are going to need. It gets a little bit confusing as we move into the new age of professionalism. Because of the multi-faceted nature of most modern businesses, there is a long list of different portfolios and resumes you must cultivate.

For the purposes of this book, I will be going over those popular three aforementioned. I am going to go over them below and what they should contain. From here, you should be able to research a little further and pull together a beautiful product.

There are multiple places online where you can buy a .PSD template for a resume. This means that you can open it up in Photoshop and truly personalize it. They are generally very cheap and well worth buying. Another reason why influencers need Photoshop!

Marketing Portfolio

A marketing portfolio contains what your resume would but is more detailed. It is a show of your ability and allows you to physically present real evidence of your talent and knowledge. Portfolios are essential tools in marketing for any professional.

Business owners will most likely be able to put one together right away. However, if you are new to all of this and looking to gain Influencer status, then you may have to wait a while before you have the information you need for a marketing portfolio.

Here is the information it should contain:

- **Cover Letter:** You should always begin with a personalized cover letter to the company. You will write this as you would any cover letter. However, the power of a portfolio is that you can reference specific examples of what you say. If you have ever heard of "show, do not tell," this is a great example of that.

- **TOC:** Because it is a much longer document than a resume, it should always have a table of contents. This should be neatly done in standard order. Looking around online will give you a better understanding of what they look like and how to format them.

- **Standard Resume:** Yes, your standard resume will be part of your marketing portfolio. This will be one page and include all of the information I will provide in the "standard resume" section below.

- **5 Recent Samples of Work:** These will be numbers and analytics pulled from projects you have worked on. It can be in relation to driving website traffic or having a fantastic engagement on social media. These numbers will indicate your success in your marketing endeavors.

You do not want to use your best examples overall, however. Keep these as the most recent that you have done but choose the best of those most recent. You want it to reflect what you are capable of right now and be honest about your successes. Faking it until you make it is great in theory, but word travels fast in the world of professionals. If you take on more than you can handle, it can end badly.

- **Awards or Special Honors:** If you have received special recognition for something in your career, include it here. This could even be features in magazines or other publications and awards which show you to be an expert in your field. You can also put letters of recommendation here, which should go at the very back.

Standard Resume

This is, hopefully, a resume we are all familiar with. Most people learn how to formulate the perfect resume while they are still in school. However, some of you may not have completed schooling. Even if you are working with a GED or without a college degree, you can absolutely make it on the social media sphere. I want to make sure that I go over how to put together a standard resume, although I will not take too much time on it.

Here is everything it contains piece by piece:

- **Cover Letter:** This will be much the same as it would be in a marketing portfolio. Your cover letter is going to be your opening for that job specifically. It should always be redone for each resume sent in so that it applies only to the job you are currently trying for. Some companies will give you a list of what they want to be answered in it, as well.

- **Contact Information:** You are going to want to include contact information for yourself. I will provide a short list below of what to include.

Full		*name*
Cell	*phone*	*number*
Professional		*E-mail*
Website		
LinkedIn		*profile*

The last one should always go on a resume because it will give them immediate access to your "breathing" resume (LinkedIn).

- **Key Skills:** These are the skills that will help you get the job done. You need to make sure you are filling in this section with the skills the best you have to offer.

- **Overview of Positions:** This will be your list of places you have worked and how long you spent there. Make sure to be concise and talk point-blank about what you did.

- **Education Information:** If you did go to college, this is where you will put your Alma Mater and the details for the degree you received.

- **Volunteer or Charity work:** While not everybody will have something to put in this section, I always recommend trying to do at least a little charity work. This is especially crucial for influencers since the general feeling people have is that they are not the type of people who do charity work.

  There are a lot of great ways you can incorporate your work as an influencer into charity work. It is highly recommendable that you do.

- **Relevant References:** Try and cultivate 5 references from people who you have worked with. It is important that you get at least one reference from an employee if you are in management.

Influencer Resume

This is a far more interesting section, and I am sure you are wondering what it is all about. If you were not already aware, influencers now have their own resume system. This allows companies to see what you are all about and what you have done at a glance. This is especially important for those who are looking to land sponsorships. You need to be able to provide official documentation talking about your expertise and experience.

- **Cover Letter:** I will not say much more about this. You get the idea. You need to make a cover letter for all resumes.

- **Contact Information:** This will be the same contact information I listed in the last section. Just make sure you are using the contact information you always use as an influencer. You should have a professional e-mail by now for your brand.

- **Social Profiles:** Since these resumes are electronic, you can put the link right in the resume. Include a link to your Twitter, Facebook, Instagram, and all the rest. Make sure that you include follower counts, current engagement rates, and all of the other analytics that is important.

- **Summary/About Me:** Write a snippet about yourself! You want your personality to shine through. After all, half of what a company is paying for sponsorship is exactly that: your personality. You want to include a nice, bright photo of yourself where you are smiling and happy. Make sure everything is on-brand so that you properly represent   yourself.

Remember, as an influencer, it is not just about scoring sponsorships or getting involved in collaborations. It is about making sure your personality and brand lines up with theirs. You cannot set out to just gobble up as many advertising deals as possible. Be patient and make sure you take on the ones you really believe in.

- **Experience:** If you have previous experience with professional social media work, or have done campaigns, this is where you will put that done. Running contests, giveaways, and more, all count. You will want to list the other collaborators and what your role was during the event.

- **Key Abilities:** This is where you will highlight all of your different abilities as an influencer. Think about what your best features are and what you are most talented for. Some influencers will also put down a list of the affiliates they would be the best working with. For example, a fitness blogger would write down a list of the best types of workouts they do or any specialized diets they have experience in.

- **Affiliations:** If you are one of those lucky people who have already gotten a sponsorship, show that loud and proud here! You will make a list of any companies you have worked within a professional capacity as an influencer. This will also help a potential sponsor see that you know what you are doing and have already gotten sponsored. It really does help your legitimacy.

That concludes the three different resumes you should have on LinkedIn. This may seem like career advice rather than advice on social media, but when it comes to LinkedIn, the two are interconnected. This is the last chapter because it is the last step on the journey to social media success. You need to build your professional presence in order to be taken seriously. It is not just about high follower counts or big engagement rates. It is about you as a person showing companies that you are to be trusted and that you have been trusted in the past.

You will know by reading those descriptions which ones you will need. You will preferably have enough information to fill out all three of them, however. That is the ultimate goal. Even if you own a business, you should always keep all three of these updated and close at hand. You never know when they may come in handy and get you out of a tight spot.

This is good information to know for your life in general, but it is especially important for the legitimacy of your brand and company. You want to make sure that people take you seriously in the world of influencing and social media.

Speaking of professionalism and being taken seriously, I want to make sure you have a few rules of etiquette for LinkedIn, as well. Again, it is far more important on this platform that you make sure you know what you are doing. You do not want to make a fool of yourself due to breaking some rules of etiquette you did not even know about. As I said, I recognize that somebody reading this may not have a strong, professional background. I also realize that you may not even have a high school diploma!

That is totally fine. This is an opportunity anybody can get in on. Even those of you who think you are already well-rounded professionals can stand to gain from this. Without further delay, here is what you need to know about what to do, and what not to do, on LinkedIn.

10 Things You Need to Do

Below, I will put all of the necessary components of interaction on LinkedIn. These will be things you need to make sure you are staying on top of. Hopefully, this will keep you on the right track and moving towards creating a large, sustainable network of people.

- **Send Thank-You Notes:** Whenever a person does something nice for you, always send them a note of thanks through LinkedIn. This is a great way to open communication with them and let them know that you appreciate them. You can always follow this up with an endorsement or by verifying some skills, too!

It is always better to send physical thank-you notes. However, LinkedIn is a great place to do that and it is more than acceptable to do so.

- **Send a "Welcome" Message:** When somebody joins your network, thank them for doing so! Make sure this is a personalized response. If they are somebody you have not met before, shoot them a message thanking them and inviting them to talk to you whenever they need to. If it is somebody you know, make it more personalized!

- **Be Prompt in Responses:** The worst thing you can do is to keep professionals waiting. They hate that. We all do, but professionals especially. Just like with any other inbox on social media, you want this one to be kept as close to completely clear as possible.

- **Personalize Your Functions:** Several different functions on LinkedIn have pre-made responses. I will always recommend that you go through and personalize them so they do not sound like a robot. You want everything to be branded; that goes for LinkedIn, too! Everything, right down to automated responses, should be personalized entirely to your brand.

- **Be Professional, Always:** First and foremost, professionalism should always be present. There are no emojis, no "text speak"; none of that. You need to make sure you are typing in complete sentences and sound well-written over a text medium. On other social media platforms, you can let loose and really go with what your brand represents. On LinkedIn, it is a different animal.

- **Content, Content, Content:** This sounds familiar, does it not? While LinkedIn is incredibly different, there are still some things that remain the same. The key to making sure your network is growing and that you are building your LinkedIn is to make sure there is content coming out consistently. I will go over some great content ideas at the end of this chapter.

- **Stay Fully Engaged:** Again, staying relevant is key. If people do not see your name for a couple of days, then you are going to fade out of memory. For LinkedIn, you want to make sure you are scrolling through at least once a day. Interact especially with those who are in your network. Do not neglect current connections in favor of making more. In this case, less is always more. Focus on the quality of the connections you make rather than the quantity.

- **Make Suggestions to Others:** If you find the content you think would be helpful or see somebody asking a question, reach out. You can do this by commenting on their posts or by messaging them directly. The best way to get people to start following you and interacting with you is to make sure that they know you are helpful.

When somebody proves that they have great connections, you want to jump on that. Make yourself "somebody to know" by always having a suggestion to make or a piece of advice to give.

- **Help Others Form Connections:** This goes hand-in-hand with the rule above. If somebody has a problem or poses a question and you cannot help, see if you know somebody who can. People will remember that you introduced them. This always looks good for you! Being helpful is always a great way to let people know that you are genuine, and a good person to have around. It is truly all about who you know.

10 Things You Need to Avoid

On the other hand, there are some things you need to avoid at all costs. These are going to be things you never want to do. Make sure you keep an eye on this list and avoid doing anything that could get you in hot water. The last thing you want is for your network to mistrust you or think badly of you!

- **Avoid Spamming:** For the love of everything good and professional, do not send spam messages. You do not want to flood people with the information they do not care about. This includes sending messages about the new blog you posted or some content you have up on your social media. LinkedIn is absolutely not the place to do this.

  Any information you send to people should be of use to them. Do not be self-serving on this platform. While there are some campaigns that involve auto-sending messages to accounts on social media platforms, this is one where you stay away from that entirely.

- **Do Not Use Scripts:** I would hope that this would go without saying. As mentioned, you should always send messages welcoming people to your network. This is helpful and opens communication between you.

144

However, it should always be personalized, as I mentioned in the "Dos" section. Do not use a script because they will absolutely spot it a mile away. These are not your average social media users. They are professionals who know every trick in the book.

- **Profile Viewing:** Did you know that with a premium subscription, you can actually see who views your profile and how many times? This is an awkward situation to be in if you go back to look at somebody's profile perhaps a few more times than you should. A lot of people do not know this, especially those who do not use LinkedIn yet.

  Keep viewing somebody's profile to a minimum for this reason.

- **Keep It Open:** This should be something you do across the board. You can lock up your LinkedIn so only a select few can see it. For the best results, however, you want to make sure everything is open. The entire point of networking is so people can check you out before they reach out. Make sure they can do this by keeping your profile open to viewing.

- **E-mails are Sacred:** There is an option to export the e-mails of your connections to your mailing list. Do not, under any circumstances or for any reason, do this. E-mails are sacred and people are trusting you to not use or sell their information. It does not matter if you are compiling a mailing list for e-mail campaigns.

Nothing you are going to do with them matters. There is no reason that can make it okay to do. In some countries, such as Canada, this is actually illegal to do. Just ignore the fact that it is even the ability of yours.

- **Do Not Request Endorsements:** Honestly, this is just tacky. Please do not ask people to endorse your skills. If you have done a great job, they will do it themselves. You can even endorse them, if you have experience with them, to try and get them to return the favor. After all, that is proper etiquette! However, at the end of the day, that endorsement is up to them.

On that note, make sure to endorse others who endorse you.

- **Do Not Request Verification:** Remember how I talked about verifying skills, and how great that looks? Do not ask people to verify them. This is just like the rule above: it looks tacky, and it puts somebody in an awkward position.

The only workaround to this is people you work with daily, or your boss, or somebody else along those lines. You can always let them know that you made a LinkedIn and ask nicely if they would endorse the skills of yours since they work with you. If you have a friendly relationship, they will probably be more than happy to help you off on the right foot.

For all others? Never, ever ask.

- **Humblebragging is a No-No:** This is a trap that many will fall into. LinkedIn can be a hot pot for humblebragging. Essentially, this when you pretend to show humility with the intention of actually bragging about yourself.

  Here is an example of humble-bragging an Influencer might make:
  "Having 100 followers instead of 10,000 as I have is such a blessing! You can really get down on their level and relate to them."

  Stay away from that. If you are going to show humility, show real humility. Nobody likes somebody who wants to brag so badly that they are willing to do it in such an underhanded way.

- **Keep Criticisms to Yourself:** If you notice somebody saying something you do not agree with, keep scrolling. While Facebook has a huge problem with constant and consistent arguing in the comments, LinkedIn does not. You are better off just leaving it alone. Do not criticize others either or give recommendations unless you are specifically asked for it.

  If somebody posted their resume, for example, do not comment on it suggesting what they could do to make it "better." Instead, just congratulate them on redoing it and tell them it looks great. If you want, you can even share it. Just be kind to others and thoughtful about your interactions.

Hopefully, you will be started off on a much better foot now that you know exactly what will be expected of you. LinkedIn can be scarier than any of the other platforms because you may not know what to expect. However, now that I have gone over everything you need to know in the beginning, I want to layout some content ideas for you. You should have everything you need in the way of creating great content as well as scheduling it.

Remember: you can schedule things to post to LinkedIn, too!

There are quite a few places you can begin with this. I would recommend scheduling something to post at least twice a day. You can cross-post content, as well. So, if you have a website, begin loading in blog posts from your website to go on your LinkedIn. Make sure to add an excerpt of some sort along with it.

However, there is much more you can do in this way. Let me share with you some of the best ideas for LinkedIn content, and how you should get started:

Long-Form Blog Posting

This is a huge source of content! It does take more time, however, so I suggest having your website up and running at this point. You will always need to have a website where you enter in blogs. This is another way to generate passive revenue through your social media accounts. Long-form simply refers to big, long blog posts that relate to your niche or field. Let me give you some examples of topics you can go over below.

- **Triumphs you have experienced recently.** While you can post snippets, which I will go over later, you should also create a great blog post to go with it. You do not actually have to have a website to do this. LinkedIn allows long-form posting with a built-in system.

- **Thoughts on the industry.** This is a great way to talk about everything and show that you have a great handle on it. Some writers talk about toxic culture and how to avoid it. Others may talk about ways to take care of yourself even while staying current and present online. It is up to you! Just brainstorm and write about what you think you will be good at.

Share Industry-Related News

It is never a bad thing to make sure people know you are aware of what is going on in your industry. Scrolling through LinkedIn, especially if you are following people and companies related to your niche, will give you great content to curate. This goes for anything from other influencing professionals sharing their own blog posts to the latest in Google Trends. The best pieces of news are below.

- **Google Trends for platforms is important.** This is something you should keep track of. Many things are influenced by Google and it is great at keeping track of what is what on the digital

- **What bigger companies or influencers are up to.** Did somebody else post about a milestone? Are they hosting a web-seminar or a workshop? Share what they are posting and give them congratulations alongside it.

- **Great things sponsors have been doing.** Any sponsor or company you want to work with should be first on your list for content curation. This puts you more on their radar and helps you cultivate a better relationship.

- **General industry trends are great.** This is not just about Google Trends. Remember how I went over the hottest trends for each platform? You want to keep up with those trends and post about them on LinkedIn to show that you are current with what is happening.

Brag Just a Little

Okay, I know I told you not to humblebrag. However, this is entirely different. It is okay to brag just a little bit if you are doing so openly. Do not try to mask it! Just post about something you have accomplished and are proud of. LinkedIn is a place to share professional triumphs, after all! People love to see that others are succeeding, and it definitely gives you the edge. If they know about your accomplishments, they are far likely to reach out for advice or follow you.

- **Small snippets of cool things you are doing.** You can post highlights of traveling you are accomplishing or any workshops you go to. It is always a great idea to attend social media and digital marketing workshops.

- **Goals and milestones you are passing.** Did you recently hit 50k followers? Brag a little bit! Post a message about what happened and how thankful you are for this opportunity. This also gives you the chance to invite people to follow you on those channels to "join the fun."

Write Tips & Tricks Articles

Short, simple, and perfect for gaining attention from others. Tips and tricks are highly sought after, especially by those new to the scene. You can also show your prowess as a social media specialist by putting out tips and tricks. This will be your own way to get others started on social media, and LinkedIn!

After all, once you are done reading this book, you will already be far more educated than most people. Show that you have the leg-up on your competitors by being the one to provide them with information on how to succeed.

- **Dos and donts for different platforms.** Again, this is something I went over in this book. Draw your inspiration from things I have gone over! That is part of showing your prowess.

- **How to get more engagement on posts.** This is another thing people are always on the look-out for. Create a little how-to segment on boosting the engagement of accounts on social media.

Write How-To Articles

These are perfect for getting your content to gain traction and, perhaps, even go viral. You should put some serious research into these, however, since they need to be well-thought-out. You want them to be legitimately helpful to those reading them. While this may seem similar to "tricks and tips," keep in mind that those will be much shorter and bulleted. How-to articles will be much longer and more in-depth. Below are some fantastic ideas for how-to articles that everybody needs to read.

- **How to grow your following.** You will have grown yourself a lovely following across platforms at this point. You are now educated on it and can offer that education to others.

- **How to start an account on social media platforms.** This is a really basic one that most people have gone over. However, it is good to have in your repertoire to make sure you have a solid listing of this style of article. Your account will have all of the posts you have made on LinkedIn, so doing a how-to for each platform will give you a lot of content in that section. Remember: it is all about content!

- **The best ways to create great content.** Alongside tips and tricks, you can also do a full article that is more in-depth on the topic. Link to your tips and tricks to drive traffic there, as well. "Cross-linking" is the practice of strategically linking your own articles in the articles you are writing. That is part of the reason you want to do similar topics to each other.

Invite Discussion in Your Connections

Do you know how calls to action are super important? This is the same on LinkedIn. By inviting discussion, you are making a call to action. People on LinkedIn absolutely love to put their two cents in. This is part of being a professional and, in a lot of cases, an intellectual.

- **Post questions about people's day.** This is a great, simple way to ask people what is going on with them. It also invites casual conversation that lets you nurture professional relationships. Sure, it is all about professionalism, but the goal is to open up communication and make sure you are building those bonds.

- **Ask about the best practices people would suggest.** Honestly, it goes for just about anything. People love, again, to give their 2 cents. It helps them "prove" themselves and justify their place on LinkedIn and as a professional. You can really ask questions about what people think

- **Ask about people's social media information.** This helps you find them and follow the others. It is a great way to network not just on LinkedIn, but to expand that networking back into your social media presence.

I recognize that LinkedIn is so incredibly different from every other platform. Hopefully, after reading these sections, you will have a great start to your profile and can begin creating, curating, and scheduling content appropriately. Honestly, when it comes down to it, LinkedIn is just another way to network with others. You just need to tackle it under a professional lens.

Once you immerse yourself and begin working towards it, you will find that it is not so scary after all.

The very last section in this book is, of course, the hottest trends related to this platform. LinkedIn is constantly shifting and changing depending on the trends in the different industries and niches. However, there are some things that will remain the same for a long time to come. Here are the best trends and fads you need to stay on top of right now:

Hot Trends on LinkedIn

- **Share Your Story:** While this has been a trend for a while, people are now really ramping it up in this area. The content I suggested you create has a few pieces related to this. Essentially, you want to play into the authenticity I mentioned in previous chapters. That is the biggest trend across all platforms right now, but especially on LinkedIn.

Tell people about the struggles you have had and how you persevered. Be open and honest about your failures and mistakes and, better yet, tell people how you overcame. Motivational speaking is becoming more and more popular in the digital sphere.

- **Lessons Learned Posts:** Again, it is all about that authenticity! You really need to focus on those things which you have learned along the way. Creating a blog post titled "Things Social Media Has Taught Me," for example, is a great place to start. You can list things out from 1 to 10 to make it more appealing and pull them in.

Aside from just sharing your story, you are really focusing on your failures and missteps. That is an important part of your journey and can be inspiring to others. It makes you seem so much more approachable and people feel more comfortable reaching out.

- **Do Presentations:** In general, presentations are a great way to go. This is really becoming popular and spreading like wildfire. How many times have you seen ads on Twitter and Instagram, and even Facebook, about seminars that people are hosting? Most will charge for this information. In the beginning, make sure you are offering it for free.

If people like the info you are sharing on social media, they will pay you when you come out with exclusive content.

- **Put Up Videos:** This goes with the above trend, but videos, in general, have been taking off. Recently, people have been posting more and more of them, some edited and interactive for your brand. Posting links to YouTube is great, but you can host videos right on LinkedIn and that is a fantastic idea.

That concludes this book on social media. I am so happy to have walked you through all of the information you need to know to get your journey started on the right foot. Remember, you can always bookmark passages you need, such as content recommendations.

This will help you sit down and create the right schedule with tips from me, and then curate and create content according to my suggestions.

Social media influencing is well within your reach. After reading this book, you are well on your way to influencing. Good luck, even though I know you are not going to need it! You have raw talent. Just keep persevering and pushing through.

In this industry, it is all about perseverance.

Conclusion

Thank you for making it through to the end of *Social Media Marketing for Beginners*. Let's hope it was informative and able to provide you with all of the tools you need to achieve your goals whatever they may be.

The next step is to begin building your empire. I do not know which road you are taking, but this book will have equipped you with the tools you need for the job. Whether you are looking to expand your business, bring in some passive revenue, or take the Influencing industry by storm, you are off to a great start.

Remember, this is the order in which I recommend that you join these networks:

- *Instagram*

- *Twitter*

- *Facebook*

- *YouTube*

- *LinkedIn*

This will give you the best chance at growing your following the correct way. You may want to switch them around, depending on which platforms are doing the best. However, in general, I find that is the order in which success comes naturally.

Keep in mind all of the things I taught you in chapter one. This is the chapter you should absolutely re-read after you are done with this book. The rest of them, I hope you highlighted or bookmarked in order to keep your place. There is a lot of information you will want to keep track of so that you can reference it as you move forward in your plans for social media success.

The world of networking through app and website platforms has never been bigger. The younger generations are more and more taking to the net and choosing to spend their time in the digital space. Because of this, e-commerce is huge and there has never been a better time to start a business. Starting out by working your way to influencer status is a great start. You can easily land a job in social media or start selling merchandise. There are so many different things that influencers can use to gain passive income through social media

Of course, the same goes for those who already have a business and need to move onto the digital space. You also may find it best to begin by making yourself an Influencer. In fact, as I mentioned, I always recommend that business owners also have their own personal accounts. There is always something to be gained by having a massive following.

Good luck on your journey, no matter which road you are taking! I know that after reading through my book, you have what you need to get what you want.

Finally, if you found this book useful in any way, a review on Amazon is always appreciated!

www.ingramcontent.com/pod-product-compliance
Lightning Source LLC
Chambersburg PA
CBHW070341220526
45467CB00001B/211